CASINO GAMBLING

CASINO GAMBLING

HOW TO BEAT THE HOUSE AT ITS OWN GAME

LEN MILLER

Revised and updated by Big Billy Holdem

BLACK DOG
& LEVENTHAL
PUBLISHERS
NEW YORK

Published by

Black Dog & Leventhal Publishers, Inc.
151 West 19th Street
New York, NY 10011

Distributed by

Workman Publishing Company
708 Broadway
New York, NY 10003

Manufactured in the United States of America

Cover and interior design by Filip Zawodnik
Illustrations by Greg Stadnyk

ISBN: 1-57912-415-1

g f e d c b

Library of Congress Cataloging-in-Publication Data is on file at
Black Dog & Leventhal Publishers, Inc.

TABLE OF CONTENTS

CRAPS: FROM BASIC TO EXPERT

Craps is the fast-moving, action-filled game that is so often identified with high rollers. As you may know, "high roller" is the name given to big-money players. Many of these $100-chip bettors walk into a craps game with a credit line ranging from $5,000 to $100,000.

The great thing about playing craps is that the $2 or $5 bettor stands right alongside the high roller and shares the fun and excitement of the game in the same manner. In many cases, the player starting out with $50 in chips and making small bets may walk away from the table with anywhere from $500 to $1,500 in profits, while the high roller may still be writing markers trying to recoup his losses.

That scenario can apply to you and your own $50 bankroll if you pay close attention to this chapter and practice what you learn.

Although you may walk up to a craps table and become befuddled by all the action going on, craps is really quite simple to learn. The game, incidentally, is always called craps: You shoot craps, you're a craps shooter, and, ironically, if you roll craps you lose!

The Roll of the Dice

Craps is a dice game played with dice. *It is a game of chance!* There is no skill in shooting craps. Each time the dice are rolled, the probabilities of any set of numbers coming out are always exactly the same.

That is your first lesson. The paragraph above cannot be disputed. So don't fight it—believe it. If a shooter makes a 7 on his first roll, and another 7 on the next roll, there is no reason to say he can't win on the third roll. The chance of rolling a 7 on any given roll is exactly six chances in 36. Significantly, the 7 comes up, or rather has a chance of coming up, on any roll more than any other number. Diagram 1-1 shows the thirty-six rolls and the odds probability of each pairing:

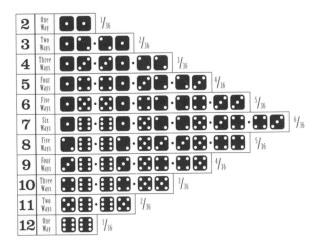

2	One Way		$^1/_{36}$
3	Two Ways		$^2/_{36}$
4	Three Ways		$^3/_{36}$
5	Four Ways		$^4/_{36}$
6	Five Ways		$^5/_{36}$
7	Six Ways		$^6/_{36}$
8	Five Ways		$^5/_{36}$
9	Four Ways		$^4/_{36}$
10	Three Ways		$^3/_{36}$
11	Two Ways		$^2/_{36}$
12	One Way		$^1/_{36}$

DIAGRAM 1-1

Actually, there are only eleven different numbers (pairings) that can be rolled. As you can see in diagram 1-1, while there is just one way to roll a 2, and only one way to roll a 12, there are two ways to make a 3 or 11, three ways for a 4 and 10, four ways to roll a 5 or 9, five ways for a 6 and 8, and six ways to make a 7.

* * *

This clearly shows the math of craps. While each roll of the dice can produce any of those eleven numbers, and although the probabilities are clearly stated, it is also true that the number 12 could come up on two consecutive rolls. If you bet a $5 chip on 12 and it came up on that roll, you would receive $150 as your payoff. If you let that amount ride—that is, bet the $150 on 12 for the next roll—and it repeated as stated above, you would receive the whopping sum of $4,500.

By the same token, betting on the 12 is something we strongly suggest not doing. It and other bets like it are too advantageous for the house, as you will learn from what you read here.

An Introduction to Craps

The game of craps is easy to learn and play. The rules are simple to follow. It's a fun game that can add considerable enjoyment to your gambling holiday. And even though most young ladies may not have played craps during their youth, casino bank craps is as much a game for women as it is for men.

The difference between a private game of craps and casino bank craps is this: In the former, there is no bank. A shooter puts some money down and another player or players *fade* him. The player is betting he will win, the *faders* betting he will lose. The shooter picks up the dice and rolls them. When rolling the dice, the same rules apply the world over. That is, the mechanics of the game are the same in a private game as they are in a casino bank game. The only material difference is that players are betting against each other.

In a casino bank game, the players place their bets and the casino bank *fades* them. In addition to covering every player's bet (*cover* has now replaced the term *fade*), the casino bank craps game offers many other types of proposition bets. These bets, along with the basic *pass* and *don't pass* bets, are explained in diagram 1-2.

As you will note, there are four people actively running the game. The *boxman*, sitting behind the table in the middle, is the boss. It is his duty to watch each roll of the dice and keep his eyes constantly on the game. The two dealers, one to each side of him, pay off the players when they win and rake in their chips when they lose. Each dealer handles all the players on his side. The table is divided by the center box of *proposition* bets and also by the *stickman*, who stands on the players' side of the table.

The players stand around the table, usually three or four at each end and four to six on either side of the stickman.

The stickman controls the action of the dice as well as the pace of the game. After seeing that all bets are down, the stickman pushes a few sets of dice to the shooter. That player selects a pair of dice and is ready to roll. The casino rules for throwing the dice are simply to roll them across the table so that they hit the wall at the opposite end. Other than that, any way you throw them is OK.

After you have thrown the dice, the action proceeds as follows:

If, on the first roll, you make a 7 or 11, you have shot a *natural*, and you win. What you win is the equivalent amount of chips you have bet on the *pass line*.

If you roll a 2, 3, or 12 on your first throw, that is called *craps*, and you lose. The dealer picks up your *pass line* bet. However, the shooter does not relinquish the dice. He continues to hold the dice until he *sevens out*.

If, on the first roll, you shoot a 4, 5, 6, 8, 9, or 10, that is your established *box point*. The object then is to keep rolling the dice until you make that number again. You lose, however, if you roll a 7 before making your box point.

* * *

Many other bets can be made, all of which are explained in diagram 1-2 (page 12).

Although casinos throughout North America abide by the basic rules, there are some differences in odds that casinos offer players. On one-roll *field* bets, for example, some casinos give 2 to 1 odds on the 2, and 3 to 1 odds on the 12. Other casinos might allow the *pass line* bettor to take double odds on the box point. If, for example, you bet $5 on the *pass line* and you rolled a 6, you would be allowed to bet $10 in back of your *pass line* bet, which would pay off at $12 for your $10 *odds* bet. Now that you know the basic rules, the dealer will be happy to inform you of any house variations.

* * *

What you have just read covers the basics of craps. If you study and learn this easy-to-follow text, you will know as much about the fundamentals of craps as a pit boss, boxman, or dealer. Most importantly, you will be an informed and knowledgeable player. The next step is to play like a pro and increase your chances of winning each time you step up to the craps table.

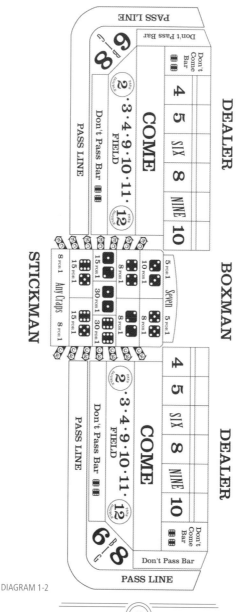

DIAGRAM 1-2

Best Betting

Once you study and become acquainted with the various kinds of wagers described in diagram 1-2, the roll-by-roll action at the craps table will become crystal-clear to you. Study this diagram, and then take note of the following comments directly related to the betting strategy recommended.

First of all, let's look at the bets you *should not* make. These are known as *proposition* bets, and they include all of the *hard way* bets. Here, the odds in favor of the casino are from over 9 percent to over 11 percent. These are bad bets, so don't make them; save your money for the good bets. The next bets not to make are the *one-roll* bets. These are 2, 3, or 12, and also 7 and 11. On these, the house edge ranges from 9 percent to over 16 percent. The other *one-roll* bet is the *field*, where the odds in favor of the house are 5½ percent.

Get Smart

That leaves us one smart area of play. In fact, it's the only form of betting that knowledgeable players use. We're talking about betting on the shooter. If you're going to bet that the dice will win, put your chips on the *pass line* directly in front of you and follow these step-by-step instructions. See diagram 1-2 for the location of the pass line.

The house percentage on this bet is a mere pittance. It is less than 1½ percent, and it will not drain your bankroll like those other bets described. This rate is reduced even further when you take full odds in back of your pass line bet. The house percentage is now reduced to two-thirds of 1 percent.

Here is an example. You bet $10 on the pass line. The shooter rolls 5 for a number. You now bet an additional $10 in back of your pass line wager, which means you are taking the odds on the point number 5.

If the shooter makes his point before rolling a 7, the pass line wins and all bettors get paid even money on their line bets. In addition, your $10 odds bet receives a payoff of $15; that's a full odds payoff of 1½:1. In all, you invested $20 and you now have $45, a net profit of $25.

If you do nothing else at the craps table except play the pass line, take the full odds every time a point is established, and bet according to the progressive money management method we're going to suggest, you'll be the smartest player at the table.

Some Money Management Tips

Here is our recommendation for that winning program:

(1) Increase your bets *only* on wins. Keep your bet at the same starting level after any loss.

(2) The amount of your starting bet is called one *unit*. Thus, if you bet a $5 chip, that is your unit. If you decide to start with a $10 bet, even though that would be two $5 chips, it would still be one unit. Each time you win, increase your bets in the following progression:

When you win your first bet, you get paid one unit. You now have two units—let it ride. Your second win will give you four units. Take one unit off, and bet three units. (You have now recovered your initial one-unit bet.) A third win gives you six units—let it ride. The fourth win gives you twelve units—take off eight units, and let four units ride. (You now have an eight-unit net profit plus a four-unit bet on the line, all winnings.) If the next bet wins, let eight units ride so that you can reap a twelve-unit net profit and still have four units in winnings on the line.

* * *

The reasoning behind this system is that if a hot hand comes up, you are showing a profit without taking a risk. Once you take off the first unit, you are betting with winnings. But in order to walk away from the table with a sizeable amount of winnings, you must bet progressively.

* * *

Remember to *never* increase your bets on a loss. If you lose your bet at any time during the progression, go back to placing only a one-unit bet. Remember, too, that the term "unit" applies to the aggregate amount of your first bet. It can be a $5 chip, or $25, or $10, as was illustrated in the example.

There is no way to guess or predict when the dice will start making passes. But as long as you stay with your one-unit bet, you will be able to conserve your bankroll until a win cycle starts. That's why we caution you against making any of those *proposition* bets—the house edge *can* and *will* eat up your bankroll.

* * *

What you've read up to this point has discussed not only the basics of craps but also some methods of betting. True, these methods have been confined to what we consider the best bet on the table; i.e., playing the pass line and playing the odds in back of your pass line bet each time a shooter establishes a point number.

Obviously, there are many other areas in which to place a bet. Learning these areas, and knowing what the house percentage is, will at least give you an intelligent choice of where to bet your money.

The more conversant one is with a game, with each and every aspect of that game, the more knowledgeable one becomes. In a word, *confidence* is what gives any player an edge. But confidence must be earned. You must be able to honestly say, "I can play with full confidence in my knowledge and ability."

Confronting the Casino

Although we have stated that you will become an expert at the game of craps just by reading and studying this text, there is also the matter of practical experience. Let's take a tour and go through the motions of entering a casino and playing at the craps table.

The casino atmosphere is responsible for a couple of known factors, both of which are pertinent to your casino visit. It's a pleasure to play and have fun in today's casinos, which feature beautiful lighting, decor, courteous people, all creating an exciting atmosphere and a general feeling of festivity.

Taking Your Time

Remember, as with all time dedicated to recreation, gambling is recreation; it is fun, it is to be enjoyed just as you would a fine dinner, a great play, a movie. We take time to plan our leisure time, our recreation. People always consider where to dine, what movie or play to see. And so should you literally create a plan when you go to a casino. It's a given—there's a large slice of luck involved in winning during a gaming visit. But success in playing games tables or slots is heightened when the player brings a bright, confident, intelligent demeanor to the casino floor. Just as this section of the craps chapter suggests, "taking your time" means . . . T-H-I-N-K.

One shouldn't run over to the table and get caught in a bad streak that will eat up an entire bankroll. We suggest that, as you walk into the casino, you acclimate yourself to the scene. Walk around. Become familiar with what's going on. Stand at a table and watch the game, go ahead and even make some mind bets. Those tables, those games—the action you see goes on continuously. What you will be gaining by these observations is a casual yet aware attitude, and possibly an enhanced discipline that is necessary to properly playing the games.

Naturally, each situation is different. Since the subject at hand is craps, let us approach the craps table and enter the game.

* * *

The first step is to take out the amount of money with which you wish to play. Your discipline must be such that you *will not* take out any more money in the event you lose the initial amount. By doing this, you will not suffer the possibility of losing all of your money. Our reasoning here is twofold: first, it's likely that, if you weren't lucky enough to hit a win streak with your initial bankroll, then taking more money out of your pocket would be throwing good money after bad; second, discipline helps you spread your money out to last you through.

Keeping that in mind, we suggest dividing your entire bankroll into playing 15 percent of it per session. Let's say you've got $500 with which to gamble over your three-day stay. That would give you $75 for this craps session. Therefore, have that amount ready when you walk up to the craps table. Give your $75 to the dealer and say, "Chips, please." You will likely receive fifteen $5 chips.

Today's casinos have different stakes at different tables; some have a $3 or $5 minimum bet. Others, in high-limit rooms, may have a $25 or $50 minimum, so pick your poison . . . but remember, T-H-I-N-K. Don't worry about the limits—they are always ample enough. With twenty-five $5 chips, you must play both aggressively and cautiously. By "aggressive," we mean just one thing: to bet progressively more on your wins. By "cautious," we mean you never double up or otherwise increase your bets on a previous loss. Caution also means to place your bets in the betting arenas that will give you the best odds.

Betting the Numbers

While it's true that craps is strictly a game of luck, it's also true that the winners are those players who *press* their luck. The word *press*, incidentally, is a term in craps: it means to add the previous win to your bet. Here's an example. If you *placed* the number 9 for $5 and a 9 was rolled, you would win $7 in profits. The dealer lets your $5 place bet ride but pays the $7 in winnings to you. At that point you may say, "Press it up," in which case the dealer extracts a $5 chip and places it on top of your existing $5 bet. You take the $2 in winnings. You now have the explanation of *press* in craps. We will, however, explain the procedure for making bets on the numbers.

Once the shooter makes a come-out roll and establishes a point number, players around the table start to make bets on the numbers. This is not to be confused with place bets. When a bettor making numbers bets says, "Place the four, five, nine, and ten for $5 each, and place the six and eight for $6 each," he is using correct terminology. In that particular case, the bettor covers all the numbers at the minimum allowable bet for a total of $32. What happens now? Every time the shooter rolls a number, that numbers bettor will receive the following payoffs: $9 winnings on a 4 or 10, $7 winnings on the 5 and 9, and $7 winnings on the $6 placed on the 6 and 8. Therefore, in each case, if you are going to press up your bet on a previous win, you know that you add $5 of your winnings on the 4, 5, 9, and 10, and $6 on the 6 and 8.

The house edge on placing the numbers is as follows: The true odds on a 4 or 10 would be 10 to 5; the house pays you 9 to 5. The true odds on a 5 or 9 are $7.50 to $5; you get paid $7. The true odds on a 6 or 8 are 6 to 5; the house is paying you $7 for your $6 bet. Incidentally, playing the numbers 6 and 8 is the best numbers bet.

The exact mathematics are as follows: When you place the 6 or 8 and receive odds of 7 to 6, the house edge is a hair above 1½ percent; when you place the 5 or 9 and receive 7 to 5, the house edge is exactly 4 percent; when you place the 4 or 10 and receive 9 to 5, the house edge is 6⅔ percent. Now you know what's against you in the house percentage when you make those numbers bets.

There is a way around the higher house odds against the 4 or 10. A bettor may *buy* the 4 or 10 and receive full odds of 2 to 1 by paying a 5 percent fee, which is called *vigorish*. For example, if you bet $100 on the 4 or 10, you actually pay $105, and if you have a win, you receive a full $200 in profits. That gives you $200 for your $105 investment, or a house edge of 4¾ percent.

Overall, betting the numbers is not a bad way of playing a house percentage, and it gives the bettor a chance to parlay winnings if those numbers keep hitting. We can say unequivocally that you *must* increase your bets on each win if you're going to walk away from the table with winning chips. The opposite is to make what are called *flat* bets. This means, for example, that you bet $5 and, win or lose, you keep betting $5; whereas in progressive betting you increase your bets and take your profits as the dice hit, if they do.

* * *

Let's see what happens to two bettors playing the numbers for the minimum of $32. One bettor is making flat bets, the other is making progressive bets, and we assume we have a decent roll going. Once the shooter establishes a point number, we make our numbers bets. During the hand, the shooter rolls a 4, which gives us a press-up to $10 plus profits of $4. Next, in rapid order, he rolls a 6 and an 8. In each case, the numbers bets were increased to $12 and we put two winning chips in the rack. Now a 5 and 9 were rolled and we again go up to $10 on each of those numbers, plus $4 more in winnings. The shooter now makes his *box point* number: After the pass line bets are paid off and the *don't pass* bets are collected, the shooter will be coming out for a new point number. At this time, we doubled all numbers that were made, which are the 4, 5, 6, 8, and 9. Our numbers bets now total $59.

Importantly, the house proclaims that, in the come-out roll, there is no action on any of the numbers bets. They do this because, in almost all cases, the players betting the numbers are also pass-line bettors. Therefore, if the shooter makes a 7 on his come-out roll, the pass-line bettors win but the numbers bets are not disturbed. To explain further, obviously a 7 in the middle of a roll wipes out all numbers bets. But in this case it has become a standard agreement that, only on the come-out roll, there is no action of any kind on the numbers bets. Of course, it also means that if the shooter's come-out roll is a 4, 5, 6, 8 , 9, or 10, there is no action on those numbers either. Just as an aside, all *come* bets would lose if the shooter rolled a 7 on his come-out. (We will go into come bets when we finish this discourse on the numbers bets.)

As it happened, our shooter rolled an 8 for a number. So, our numbers bets are back in action. He rolls a 5, which gives us a $14 payoff. Now, on our first win, we pressed up the amount we won, but on subsequent wins we are going to take some profits. The dealer pays you $14 for your $10 on 5. You take $9 and leave $5, saying, "Press $5 more." The shooter rolls a 6, you get $14, take $8 in profits and press up another $6. He rolls a 4, which gives us an $18 payoff. Again we press up $5 and put $13 in profits in the rack. Now he comes back with another 5. Our $15 bet gives us $21 in profits. This time we're going to move up to $25 on 5. We still have $11 in profits from the $21 payoff, which we add to our rack.

Taking some profits and yet increasing our bets is the only way to make money on a lucky roll. Just think of it: If a 5 is rolled again, we will get a $35 winning payoff. That's $3 more than our initial $32 bet. And when the dice are making numbers this can all happen.

* * *

Let's continue with our scenario. Our lucky shooter makes his 8, which gives us a $14 payoff. We take $8 in profits and press number 8 up to $18. The shooter makes a come-out roll, and this time it's a 7 and all pass-line bettors win. Back he comes with another 7 and, luckily for us, our numbers bets are not affected. Now the same shooter comes back with a 10 for his point number. Since this is a come-out roll, the numbers bets are not working. But on the next roll they are. He then rolls a 5, which does in fact give us that $35 win, and we take this, letting the same $25 numbers bets stand. Moving all bets up to the $25 level is a worthwhile goal when starting with a $5 minimum bet. We now take the $35 in profits and let the $25 bet stand. Next, an 8 is rolled, which gives us a $21 payoff. We take $15 in profits and press up $6 to make it a $24 number 8. Our existing $10 bet on 9 gives us a $14 payoff. We press up $5 and take $9 in profits. Back comes another 9. With $21 in profits, we press that 9 up to our $25 level, and take $11 in profits. The shooter rolls another 5, which gives us $35 more to add to our rack. And then the inevitable: Up comes a 7 and we lose all bets.

* * *

Well, it was a decent roll and, when we add up our winnings, we should have something to show for it. Incidentally, although we started with a $32 across-the-board numbers bet, we had a total of $112 left on those numbers when the shooter sevened out. However, here is what we won by making progressive bets: $164. And here is what was won by the flat bet player: $109. He took his profits each time the same numbers were made, and when the shooter sevened out, he still had the same $32 on the line.

Each time a number is made after you've *pressed* your bets up to the $25 mark, you are taking profits of $45 for a 4 or 10, $35 for a 5 or 9, and $28 for your $24 bet on the 6 and 8.

CRAPS TERMINOLOGY

ANY CRAPS—A one-toss bet on all the craps numbers with one unit, or group of units, bet on the 2, 3, 12. Payoff is 7:1.

ANY SEVEN—A one-toss bet on any of the possible combinations of 7. Payoff is 4:1.

BANKROLL—A player's total amount of betting money. Many players divide their bankrolls into smaller increments to extend their betting ability.

BARRED NUMBER—Can be either the 2 or 12. Creates a *standoff* or *push* when betting *don't pass* or *don't come*. In a standoff or push, neither you nor the casino wins any money; your bet is unaffected.

BET NUMBERS ACROSS—A group of five bets on all the place numbers *other than the point number.*

BIG 6 or BIG 8—A bet made on either 6 or 8 that it will be rolled before a 7 comes up. Pays 1:1.

BOX POINT—Shooter's number: 4, 5, 6, 8, 9, or 10.

BOXMAN—The casino employee who supervises the craps game and deposits money into the drop-box.

BUY BET—A place bet made at true odds rather than at place odds. Carries a 5 percent fee.

CHOP—A term that designates dice action of win-lose, win-lose, win-lose, etc.

COME BET—An even-money bet that is exactly the same as a *pass line* bet, *after* the shooter's point is established.

COME-OUT ROLL—The shooter's initial throw of the dice after a *pass line* decision.

CRAPS—Common name for the game of dice. Also the name given to the toss of 2, 3, or 12.

CRAPS/ELEVEN—The name used to indicate bets in the specially marked area on either *any craps* or *eleven.*

DON'T COME—An even-money bet that the shooter *will not* toss his point again before tossing a 7. The same as *don't pass* bets, after the shooter's point is established.

DON'T PASS—An even-money bet that the shooter *will not* toss his point number again before tossing a 7. The same as *don't come*, except that the shooter's point is the point number for the entire table.

DOUBLE ODDS—A bet permitted in some casinos in which the player takes an *odds bet* at twice his original wager on the line.

EASY NUMBER—Any even number that appears in any combination other than as an actual pair, e.g., 1 and 3 versus 2 and 2.

FIELD BET—A one-toss bet that 2, 3, 4, 9, 10, 11, or 12 will be the next roll of the dice. (Some layouts use 5 instead of 9; some pay double or triple on either 2 or 12.)

FLAT BETS—The type of wagers in which the player bets the same amount on each roll, win or lose.

FREE ODDS—A bet on true odds permitted with *pass* and *come* bets. Unlike *buy* bets, these do not carry a 5 percent *vigorish* charge.

FRONT LINE—The same as *pass line*.

FULL ODDS—The correct odds.

HARD NUMBER—An even number that appears exactly as a pair. Two 2s is known as *hard four*.

HARDWAY BETS—Bets made, in a specifically marked area, on an even number, that it will appear exactly as a pair. Payoffs are for greater amounts than if the number appeared as any other combination.

HIGH/LOW—A one-toss bet on both the 2 and the 12, with two units bet. Payoff is 30:1 (units).

HIGH ROLLERS—Players who have relatively large amounts of money with which to play.

HORN BET—A four-unit bet that covers all three of the craps numbers (2, 3, 12) and also the 11.

HOT HAND—A succession of passes.

HOUSE—The casino; the management.

INSIDE BETS—A *place bet* on 5, 6, 8, and 9.

LAY BET—A *place bet* made that the shooter will toss a 7 before the number bet on. Player must wager more than he expects to win. A *lay bet* is a *don't place* bet at true odds.

LAY ODDS—An additional bet that allows the *don't pass* and *don't come* bettors to give, rather than take, true odds on their bets.

LAYOUT—The physical playing area in any game, usually printed on felt in the center of all tables.

NATURAL—A 7 or 11 on the *come-out* roll.

ODDS BET—An additional bet that can be made by players having *pass line*, *come*, *don't pass*, or *don't come* bets, that the shooter will make his point. Paid at correct odds, or *full odds*.

OFF—A term indicating that bets are *not working*.

ON—A term indicating that bets *are working*.

ONE-ROLL BET—A bet decided on the next roll; as *the field*, 7, 11, or *any craps*.

OUTSIDE BETS—A *place* bet on 4, 5, 9 and 10.

PAIRINGS—The two numerals that come up together on a pair of dice.

PASS—A winning decision for pass-line bettors.

PASS-LINE BET—An even-money bet that the shooter will make his point again, before tossing a 7. The same as a *come* bet, except that the shooter's point is the point number for the entire table.

PERCENTAGE—In gambling, the hidden or direct charge made by the casino.

PIT BOSS—The supervisor of the gaming tables.

PLACE BETS—Numbered boxes in which the player wagers that any one of the numbers 4, 5, 6, 8, 9 or 10 will come up before a 7.

POINT NUMBER—In a come-out toss, the number that is other than 2, 3, 7, 11, or 12. That number becomes the point number for every player on *pass* or *don't pass*, and remains until a decision is tossed.

PRESS UP—To add to the bet with winnings from the previous roll.

PROPOSITION BET—A one-toss bet on any of the three available craps numbers, the 7, the 11, or *any craps* (a combination of the three craps).

ROLL—To throw the dice; a throw of the dice.

SEVEN OUT—When a shooter throws a 7 and loses, after establishing a point.

SHOOTER—The player who is currently rolling the dice.

STICK—A curved stick, which looks like a hockey stick, used by the stickman to manipulate the dice.

STICKMAN—The dealer in the center of the craps table who uses the stick to control the dice action, and the pace of the game.

TABLE LIMITS—Smallest and largest bets permitted at the table.

THREE-WAY CRAPS—A one-toss bet on each of the three craps numbers, with three units bet. Payoff is as shown on the layout *for the number tossed*.

TOSS—A single throw of the dice.

UNIT—Any fixed quantity, when used in describing types of bets or systems.

VIGORISH—A 5 percent fee paid on a *numbers* bet, which guarantees the player full odds on the bet.

WORKING—A term used to imply that a bet is in full force and effect, even though the entire table may not be in effect at the time. Reverse is *not working*, which implies that for a given period of time the bet is *not* in full force and effect.

WRONG BETTOR—A person wagering that the dice lose; a *don't pass line* bettor.

2

BLACKJACK, OR "21": BASIC STRATEGY AND MONEY MANAGEMENT

In the beginning, craps was the leading game in the casino. Before you ask why, it is because, during World War II, it was the quickest, not to mention the easiest, game of chance (read that as "gambling pastime") to cook up.

Military rules forbade gambling on base and on the field. A deck of cards could be difficult to hide should an officer suddenly appear. A GI could swallow a pair of dice, if he had to.

Blackjack wasn't played—who'd be the banker? Get the picture?

When the boys came home, the game they remembered most was craps, so naturally they gravitated to the table.

Eventually, looking for a place to sit—and play—they discovered the blackjack stands.

The rest, as they say, is history. Today blackjack is the favorite casino table game for men and women. A share of the game's popularity can be attributed to the scores of articles about the skills of the game; in fact, it's reputed to be the one game in which the "house" doesn't have a decided edge over the player.

Rather than being a game based strictly on chance, blackjack has more than a modicum of skill attached to it.

When a game presents options for the player, then decision-making moves come into play—skillful or not.

In blackjack all the options are open to the player, and none to the dealer. It becomes a matter of the player making what should be the right decisions. Those decisions to be remembered come from case histories of situations for each of the many different types of hands that are dealt.

After you finish this chapter you will have learned not only the rules and playing procedures but also a basic strategy for blackjack.

Learning Blackjack

The first step, of course, in playing any game intelligently is the following: Know the basic rules. It must be pointed out that these rules are *typical*, not universal. You will find slight variations in some casinos in North America and overseas.

The player attempts to obtain a total of cards equal to or less than 21—as long as the player's total is higher than the dealer's. If the total is higher than 21, the player busts, automatically losing the hand, even if the dealer subsequently busts as well.

Number of Players

One to seven players play against a house dealer. The players do *not* play against one another, but each plays against the dealer. Thus, other players' hands and the actions they take have no direct bearing on your hand and your play.

Number of Cards

The dealer uses from one to eight 52-card decks. With one or two decks, he deals by hand; with more decks, he deals from a *shoe*. While the rules of the game remain the same however many decks are used, you have the best advantage in single-deck or double-deck play.

The Shuffle and Cut

The cards are shuffled thoroughly by the dealer and cut by one of the players, usually by inserting a joker or blank card into the pack at the place where it is to be cut. After the cut, the top card is normally *burned* (discarded) in such a way that the player cannot see its value. In multiple-deck games, after the decks are placed in the shoe, it is general practice to place the blank card about three-fourths of the way back in the pack, which signals the point at which a new shuffle is generally made.

Betting

All players place their bets in front of them, generally in a small circle or rectangle on the felt, *before* any cards are dealt. (See diagram 2-1.) A player may play more than one hand, but must usually place twice the minimum wager on each hand if playing two hands, and six times the minimum wager on each hand if playing three hands.

Minimum bets vary from casino to casino. Some are as low

BLACKJACK PAYS 3 TO 2
Dealer must draw to 16 and stand on 17
Insurance pays 2 to 1 • Insurance pays 2 to 1 • Insurance pays 2 to 1

DIAGRAM 2-1

as $1, others roam from $5 to $25. In high-limit rooms within a casino, the maximum could jump to $3,000. Except for player's blackjack and insurance (discussed under "Player's Options," page 30), all bets pay even money—$1 paid for a $1 bet. In the case of a tie, or *push*, between the player and the dealer, the bet is a standoff and no money changes hands.

The Deal

Starting at his left, the dealer gives each player a card in turn and then gives himself a card. He repeats this procedure. One of the dealer's cards is dealt face up and the other face down. The players' cards are dealt either all face up or all face down. Whether they are face up or face down makes absolutely no difference; in fact, the beginner is better off playing an up game, where he can see all the cards from the start and where other people and even the dealer might be willing to advise him.

The Value of the Cards

All the picture cards—jack, queen, king—count as 10. All the other cards count as their face value except the ace, which, at the player's option, may count as 1 or 11. For example, if a player draws 6, 4, ace, he would clearly count his ace as 11 to make 21; on the other hand, if he drew 6, 7, ace, he would count the ace as 1 for a total of 14.

Soft Hands and Hard Hands

When a hand contains an ace, which may be counted as 11 instead of 1, without the total exceeding 21, that hand is referred to as a *soft* hand. Any other kind of hand is referred to as a *hard* hand. For example, a hand containing ace, 7 is considered to be a soft 18. A hand containing 10, 8 would be a hard 18. A hand containing ace, 7, 10 would also be a hard 18, since the ace cannot count as 11 without the total exceeding 21.

Blackjack

When the player or the dealer is dealt an ace and a 10-value card (a 10, jack, queen, or king) as his *first* two cards, he has a blackjack, or *natural*, which is an automatic winner. When the player receives this hand, he turns over his cards immediately; and when his turn comes, he is paid at the rate of 3 to 2, or 1½ times his wager.

Remember, to get paid at this rate of 3 to 2, the player must achieve 21 with his *first two* cards. All later totals of 21 pay only even money when they win. When the dealer has a natural 21 on his first two cards, he immediately collects all wagers except in the case of a player's blackjack, which is considered a tie or push.

The Draw

Starting with the player on the dealer's left, each player may elect to *stand*—that is, draw no additional cards—or *hit*, *split*, *double down*, or *surrender* his hand. He generally signals that he wants to stand (also called *staying pat* or *sticking*) by placing his cards under his wager. In face-up games, where the cards aren't touched, he indicates standing by placing his palm down on the table.

A player may continue to draw cards to his hand, one at a time, by calling for a *hit* (an additional card) until he chooses to stand or until he busts with a total exceeding 21. The player generally signals a hit by scratching his cards toward him against the felt or, in face-up games, by scratching the felt with his finger.

When the player busts, he automatically loses his bet on that hand and must turn his cards face up immediately, at which time the dealer collects his bet and his cards. This is the *only* advantage the dealer has over a good player. That is, he wins when a player busts even if he subsequently busts as well.

The Dealer's Strategy

The dealer really employs no strategy, for his play is determined automatically by the rules of the game. If his initial hand totals 17, 18, 19, or 20, he *must* stand. After the players have drawn, he pays all hands that are higher than his, collects from all hands that are lower, and declares a tie with all hands of equal value. If the dealer has a total of 16 or less, he *must* continue to hit his hand until it totals at least 17 or until he busts. He cannot hit a hand that totals 17, unless the casino has a rule that the dealer must hit on a "soft 17," meaning an ace and a six—which could be counted as a 7, or a 17. Remember, any hand with an ace and a card with a value of less than ten is considered "soft."

Dealers must take a hit on a soft 17.

This hit on a soft 17 is slightly disadvantageous to the player, like a little over one percentage point.

Now, should you, as a player, ever come across a game where the dealer wins all ties, give it up, leave the building, as you are giving the house another nine-point advantage.

Player's Options

In addition to drawing additional cards, the player has several options that are not available to the dealer. These are *splitting pairs*, *doubling down*, *taking insurance*, and *surrendering*. It is with regard to these options that you are most likely to find variations from one locale to another and even from one casino to another.

Splitting pairs. If the player has two cards of the same denomination—that is, two aces, 2s, 9s, and so on—he may choose to turn them face up and put up an amount of money equal to his original bet, playing each card as a separate hand. Ten-value cards may also be split. Some casinos require that they be of the same order—that is, two jacks, not a jack and a king. Most casinos, however, consider all 10-value cards to be pairs. Except for aces, a player may draw to each new hand as often as he wishes until he decides to stand or until he busts. However, because they are such potent cards, the house allows the player only one card, dealt face down, for each of his aces.

Finally—and again with the exception of aces—if the first card the player draws to either hand after splitting is of the same denomination as the split card, in effect making another pair, he may split again and bet another amount equal to his original wager, and he may continue to do so each time he makes an additional pair.

Doubling down. When, after receiving his first two cards, a player feels he has a good hand that will become a very good hand with one additional card, he may turn his two cards face up, wager any additional amount up to his original bet, and receive one and *only one* additional card, usually dealt down. (Normally, if the hand is worth doubling at all, you should bet the full amount to which you are entitled.)

Some casinos permit doubling down only with a two-card total of 10 or 11. Others do so with 9,10, or 11, while many permit doubling down with any two-card hand. When one of the two cards is an ace, it is referred to as *soft doubling*, since the player has a soft hand.

Insurance. When the dealer's face-up card is an ace, many casinos offer the player a side bet as to whether or not the dealer has a 10-value card in the hole—and therefore a natural and automatic winner. Any time he has an ace showing, the dealer must offer this *insurance* bet before he looks at his hole card.

Insurance is paid at the rate of two units for one bet, and the player can bet up to one-half his original bet. If the dealer has a 10 in the hole—and hence a blackjack—the player loses his original bet (assuming he didn't also have a blackjack) and wins the insurance side bet. If the dealer does not have a 10-value in the hole, the player loses the insurance bet and continues to play his hand as he would normally.

Veteran blackjack players welcome the opportunity to take

insurance—when the cards on the table, and the cards that have gone before, signal the possibility that the dealer has a blackjack, those players will buy insurance.

Remember, in blackjack, as in all "skill" games at a casino, *one size does not fit all*. There are options to all blackjack decisions. In general, insurance is not a sound wager.

Surrendering. Many casinos do not have this option, but many do. It works like this: When a player looks at his hand and the dealer's face-up card and decides that he has the worst of it, he may throw in his hand before drawing any other cards and surrender half of his original bet.

This is an option that an advanced player understands, but if you, the reader, are rather new to the game, it is best to be passed upon—until you feel you're no longer a rookie at the table.

These are the basic rules for playing casino blackjack. Once you have mastered them, you are ready to learn basic strategy, which is a method of deciding whether to hit, stand, double down, or split a pair on the basis of mathematical probability.

Basic strategy varies according to the number of decks in play. Because so many single-, double-, four-, six-, and eight-deck games have become common, we present in diagram 2-2 a basic strategy chart for four decks as developed by the blackjack expert Stanley Roberts.

DIAGRAM 2-2

HARD STANDING STRATEGY:	
Stand on…	…when the dealer's up card is
13 or more	2, 3
12 or more	4, 5, 6
17 or more	7, 8, 9, 10, A
SOFT STANDING STRATEGY:	
Stand on…	…when the dealer's up card is
Soft 18 or more	2, 3, 4, 5, 6, 7, 8, 9, 10
Soft 19 or more	9, 10, A

You should hit any soft total of less than 18 whatever the dealer's up card is.

HARD DOUBLING STRATEGY:	
Double down on…	…when the dealer's up card is
11	2, 3, 4, 5, 6, 7, 8, 9, 10
10	2, 3, 4, 5, 6, 7, 8, 9
9	3, 4, 5, 6

Never double down on a hard total of 8 or less or on a hard total of 12 or more.

SOFT DOUBLING STRATEGY:	
Double down on…	…when the dealer's up card is
A, 7	3, 4, 5, 6
A, 6	3, 4, 5, 6
A, 5 and A, 4	4, 5, 6

With a soft total of 19 or more, you should never double down but instead follow basic strategy for soft standing.

PAIR SPLITTING STRATEGY:	
NEVER split 4, 4; 5, 5; 10, 10.	ALWAYS split A, A; 8, 8.
Split the following…	…when the dealer's up card is
9, 9	2, 3, 4, 5, 6, *, 8, 9
7, 7	2, 3, 4, 5, 6, 7
6, 6	3, 4, 5, 6
3, 3	4, 5, 6, 7
2, 2	4, 5, 6, 7

*Note that you do not split 9s when the dealer's up card is a 7.

NEVER TAKE INSURANCE

BLACKJACK TERMINOLOGY

BASIC STRATEGY—A computer-developed method for playing blackjack—without keeping track of the cards—that may be easily memorized by a player.

BLACKJACK—A popular betting game in which the bettor is dealt two cards, either face up or face down; the dealer has one face-up and one face-down card. The object of the game is to have cards totaling 21—or as close to 21 as possible without going over, and coming closer to 21 than the dealer. A score of 21, when dealt an ace with a 10 or a picture card, is called *blackjack*.

BREAKING HAND—A hand that will *break* (go over 21) with a one-card draw, such as a hard 12, 13, 14, 15, or 16. Also called a *stiff*.

BURNED—Discarded; what is done with the top card after the deck is cut so that the player can't see its value.

BUSTED—To overdraw to a total greater than 21; an immediate losing hand.

COUNTING—The ability of a player to keep an accurate mental record of the cards that have been played. Can allow players to have a relatively good idea of which cards remain in the shoe.

DOUBLING DOWN—An option in which the player, feeling he has a good hand, which will win with one more card, turns his two cards face up and adds to his bet by as much as his original bet. This gets him *one* additional card.

DRAW—To obtain additional cards to the original two cards.

FACE CARD—King, queen, jack.

FIRST BASE—The first seat at the blackjack table, immediately to the left of the dealer.

HARD COUNT—The true face value of the cards being played with.

HARD HAND—A hand without an ace, or one with an ace that can be counted only one way (for example, an ace, 6, and 9).

HIT—To add another card to a player's hand. The player asks the dealer for another card by saying or signaling "Hit me."

HOLE CARD—The dealer's face-down card.

INSURANCE—A side bet offered to the player by the house, when the dealer's face-up card is an ace, that the dealer has a 10 as his hole card, making blackjack. Pays 2:1.

MONEY MANAGEMENT—The manipulation of increments of one's bankroll in betting, the better to overcome adverse house percentages.

NATURAL—A total of 21 in only two cards. Automatic winner, pays 3 to 2.

PIT BOSS—The person in charge of the blackjack games.

PRESS—To increase the size of the subsequent wager.

PUSH—A tie between the dealer and the player in which no money changes hands; a standoff.

SHOE—A dealing device for multiple-deck games.

SOFT HAND—A hand with an ace that can be counted optionally as 11; for example, an ace and a 7, which can be counted as totaling 8 or 18.

SPLITTING PAIRS—An option the player has with two original cards of the same denomination (4s, 8s, etc.) of splitting the two cards and playing each hand individually.

STAND—What a player does when he is satisfied with his existing cards and stays with his hand as is.

SURRENDER—The ability of the player to give up only half his bet when it is apparent that there is no way that he can beat the dealer. Must be done before any cards are drawn. Available only in certain casinos.

THIRD BASE—Last seat at the blackjack table, immediately to the right of the dealer.

TOKE—The tip or gratuity given to dealers by players.

"21"—Another name for the game of blackjack. Also, the winning total in blackjack.

UP CARD—The dealer's face-up card.

SLOTS: A NEW LOOK AT PROGRESSIVE SLOT MACHINES

The task of getting ahead of the world of slot machines is not an easy one. As a matter of fact, many visitors to casinos, experienced players among them, consider the learning curve to the play, and an understanding of slots, to be the hardest job of all. The first decision the player should make is, "What is my goal, to go after those big, life-changing payoffs, the multimillion dollar wide-area progressive jackpots?

Or, "Do I want to have a frequency of hits, of payoffs?"

What do you, as a player, want from your visit to the slot section at the casino? Besides the fun and enjoyment—which is what a casino visit is intended to be: recreation. But being better informed adds to the enjoyment. So, let's look at today's slots.

Read the Machine

It is said that over 75 percent of the people visiting a casino, first-timers or not, are constantly overwhelmed by the number and variety of slot machines on the casino floor.

They see the flashing lights, the whirling neon signs above banks of slots, along with the ambient sounds each machine emits, not to mention the crash of tokens falling into the *tubs* (even though many, many casinos have long since forsaken coins and tokens for "Ticket-In, Ticket-Out" machines . . . which means patrons are hearing the sound effects of coins falling into hoppers).

It's no wonder so many confess, "I don't know which machine to play. It's so confusing."

Well then, stop. Stop and relax. The first thing a person should do is simply stop, take a breath, and just walk around.

Where is it written that you have to rush to a machine and start stuffing money into the bill acceptor?

The first rule of slot play is slow down, walk around, don't make a sound . . . (repeat this four or five times).

See which machines are attracting the crowd. Find yourself a place to settle in and then, before you touch your money, *make sure you know how to read the machine.*

First, not all machines are the same. Yes, they're the same inside, just as you and I are the same inside: We have a heart, a liver, a set of lungs, and, believe it or not, each of us carries around a brain. Whether we use it or not is a subject of great debate.

If you are going to play the slots as part of your casino visit, and you wish to play for a while and, possibly, make a few dollars, then why not use your brain by *reading the slot machine*?

You start by reading the payout schedule at the front of the machine. Do that and you'll quickly discover that all machines are not alike. Payout schedules will help you separate the good from the indifferent.

Wait, the next-first-thing-to-check-on is: "How much does it cost me to play this machine?" Find the denomination. You may discover that it's multi-denominational, meaning it'll take nickels, dimes, quarters, dollars, etc.

Believe it or not, this is the most frequent error slot players make—thinking they're going to play one denomination only to discover they're sitting in the wrong stool. Look before you leap—isn't that what Nick the Greek once said?

Now, after reading the payout schedules, and remembering to check out the cost of playing the machine—per spin, that is—we go in search of the right type of machine we wish to play. There are several:

The Multiplier. A Multiplier is the machine that will pay out for a certain symbol, or icon, like a bell, an orange, or a monkey face. Then the number of coins played multiplies the payout. So, if the machine pays five coins for three bells when you play one coin, it *should* pay ten for the second coin played, and fifteen for the third. Another thing to remember: This machine does not penalize you for not playing maximum coins—that is why it is important to read pay schedules. If you like to play one coin at a time, and enjoy your visit to the casino for a while, then this is your machine.

The Bonus Multiplier. This machine goes about its business exactly as the Multiplier above, except it offers a bonus when you play maximum coins and hit the jackpot. Let's say Three Roses may pay one thousand for one coin, two thousand for two coins, and ten thousand for maximum coins. What you need to figure out is whether the bonus is worth the extra coin.

Multiple Payline. These are the machines that have more than one line of play. Each coin activates a given line. Now, if you hit a winner on a line that *has not been activated*, you win nothing. Again, read the machine, find out how many lines to play, pay, and win. Anywhere from three, five, nine, and into the twenties.

Buy-a-Pay. These machines are a lot like a legal brief: You'd better push the help button on these machines and read all the information available. These machines want you to know that each coin activates a different payout. And you always need maximum coins played to get in on the biggest jackpot. Example: Say a machine has three different icons—a bear, an owl, and a lion. You can collect by playing one or two coins—small amounts. If you hit the jackpot playing one of these machines with only one coin, you don't win a thing. Play these machines only with maximum coins. Again, read the machine, all of it.

Progressive Slots. The progressive slot will take a certain percentage of money played and add it to the pool, the pot that makes up the *progressive jackpot*. Progressive slot jackpots are built by several casinos being linked together, forming a network of certain machines, thus building life-changing sums of money. The Wheel of Fortune slots are a good example. Crossing several jurisdictions, scores of slots are stitched together to form a wide-area "Wheel of Fortune" opportunity for a player to win several million dollars—and it happens frequently. Keep in mind, however, that the payback percentage on progressives is lowered to allow the building of the big payday.

Besides the wide-area progressive slot offerings, several casinos get together, within a state or a close geographic area, and offer regional progressive jackpots; and many casinos have in-house progressive jackpots. This is where the jackpot is built up by players in that particular casino. Again, read the machine, and always, when in doubt, talk to a slot supervisor. All casinos have slot supervisors on the floor, at all times. They are there to answer questions and offer advice and counsel.

Remember, though, that all the slot machines have all the information you need on the front of the machine, or on the screen.

Look for the help button, and take a moment to read the machine. Again, if you can't locate the info, call for a slot supervisor. The more you know, the further you'll go.

Some Systems—Simple Strategies

Two methods, or strategies, are offered. The first one is called "The Percentage Play Way."

You are asked to play a fixed percentage of your starting bankroll for each play, or button push, or pull of the handle. OK. Let's say we've set aside $100 for today's slot play. You've picked a $1 machine. Your fixed percentage is 5 percent. That means you will bet 5 percent of the $100 on your first pull—that's $5, maximum, coins in the machine. If you win on the first pull, you continue to play at 5 percent of the winnings plus the original $100. If you lose, your 5 percent becomes less than 5 coins, down from the maximum coins venture. Win or lose, the percentage remains the same; only the amount of the investment changes.

Now then, the question becomes, "When do I quit?"

If you're losing, you quit when you've lost half of your original stake. If you're winning, you quit when your last eight pulls have returned zero.

If you're down to half of the original bankroll, consider moving to a penny machine, where you can control the amount of the wager—from a nickel to a buck. Or call it a day and head for the couch.

The Run-Through System

This is as easy as it gets: Take your bankroll, say $25, and run it through the machine just one time.

Do not, we repeat, do not replay any coins or credits you have won.

After you've played your original bankroll through the machine, take whatever credits are on the machine and quit. You may have less than the original roll, but you'll be walking out of the joint with some money, if not a jackpot.

Note: Here common sense dictates that if the machine seems to be going through a good-to-warm cycle, and you're ahead of the game from the initial session, you could play your "winnings" through the machine one more time.

After that, playing the machine becomes somewhat of a risky affair.

Facts on Slots

Remember, across America there is gambling in all fifty states except two—Utah and Hawaii.

Minimum slot machine payback percentages are programmed, yes, programmed, by the statutes of the states in which they are located—including Indian casinos that have signed compacts with their respective states. These percentages are between the low of 80 percent minimum payback and the maximum high of 99 percent.

Today's slot machines are driven by microchip processors that incorporate random-number generators. The chip drives the generator continually—whether the machine is being played or not. The brain of the machine is continually at work, 24/7, generating combinations. When your coin comes into the machine, you simply get to see this "brain" at work. This is merely a "courtesy" of the machine, allowing you to see just what is going on. You and I, as players, do not affect the final outcome, the last look.

The Solution, the Answer, the Secret

Everything comes down to the power of two: Money Management and Discipline.

Set your bankroll to coincide with the amount of time you want to spend in the casino playing and eating and having fun.

Have the discipline to do just that. Quit when the time comes, win or lose.

SLOT MACHINE TERMINOLOGY

DPSM—Double Progressive Slot Machine. A slot machine with two *progressive jackpots*, a larger one and a smaller one, with a lit arrow that alternates between them as coins are dropped into the machine.

GRAPHICS—The printed pictures of fruit, sevens, and other symbols on the reels of the slot machine.

JACKPOT—The highest prize to be won with the machine; usually, to obtain the *jackpot* three bars or sevens must be lined up.

ONE-ARMED BANDIT—The original slang term for slot machines on which players would pull a handle to set the reels spinning; "bandit" refers to the low-win percentages of some of these machines.

PROGRESSIVE SLOTS—The type of slot machines that feature *jackpots* that grow larger as more coins are fed into them.

VIDEO POKER: SOMETHING MORE THAN A SLOT MACHINE

Video poker provides decision-making action for your nickels, quarters, and dollars. This computer-generated card game follows the guidelines and rules of poker. A royal flush is the highest hand you can get; that hand wins the top prize, too. A pair of jacks is the lowest hand that will win a prize. In most cases, you get your bet back if your hand winds up with a pair of jacks, queens, kings, or aces. Two pairs of anything will get you a 2:1 payoff. Three of a kinds are worth 3:1. A straight, any size, wins 4:1. A flush nets 5:1, and a full house is good for 8:1.

Now we move up to the big time. Any four of a kind wins 25:1. A straight flush wins 50:1. And a top prize of 250:1 is awarded for a royal flush.

A Show of Hands

Here's a display of those hands mentioned and what each one looks like:

Any one of these picture pairs wins even money.

Any two pairs (regardless of size) win 3:1.

Any three of a kind wins 3:1.

This is a straight. All five cards must be in any continuous form starting with A, 2, 3, 4, or 5 and continuing up to 9, 10, J, Q, K, A. Any straight wins 4:1.

This is a flush. Any five cards of the same suit make a flush. It pays 5:1.

This is a full house. Any three of a kind together with any two of a kind make a full house. This pays off at 8:1.

Any four of a kind wins 25:1.

This is a straight flush. It's the same as a straight, but all five continuous cards must be in the same suit: spades, hearts, clubs, or diamonds. This hand pays 50:1.

This is the top hand—a royal flush in any suit. As you can see, this is also a straight flush, but it's the highest straight flush, 10 to the ace. You'll win 250:1 on this hand, plus the jackpot prize if you play five coins.

Spending and Choosing

The best video poker machines to play are those that offer a jackpot prize in addition to your regular payoff. You get this bonus when you play five coins each game.

When playing *any* slot machine, you are obviously hoping to win the largest payoff the machine provides. You get this only when you play the maximum number: five coins. When you play five quarters and hit a full house, for example, your 8 to 1 odds will give you a total return of 40 quarters or a *net* win of $8.75. But when your winning hand also provides a bonus jackpot, you'll win that much more. So, always play the maximum amount, five coins, whether they be quarters or dollars.

When you drop your coins into the slot, five video windows will electronically go into motion and then stop. What you'll see then are five cards, each randomly selected from a deck of fifty-two cards. This is your five-card hand, and you have the option of holding any of these cards or discarding one or more. The cards you discard will be replaced by new cards, which will give you your final hand.

Here is a simple example:

That's the hand you were dealt. You must now decide which cards to hold and which to discard. In this instance, the obvious choice is to hold the pair of kings and discard the other three cards. You'll then be dealt three new cards, which could conceivably give you one or two more kings, another pair, or even three of a kind.

The Video Difference

That hand also illustrates something else. Video poker differs from live poker in that you are not competing against other players. If this were a poker game played around a table with other players, it would be wise to hold the ace as a "kicker," discarding the 4 and 2, and drawing just two cards. That logic applies because you must beat your opponents in order to win. Drawing another ace could give you a high hand, with three of a kind or even something better.

In video poker *any* size pairs—three of a kind, straights, or flushes—win, regardless of their size. But in a live game, a larger-size flush or straight beats the smaller cards. A pair of aces beats a pair of kings, and so forth.

There are other differences between playing video poker and playing in a live game. There is no bluffing, no raising, and no other form of psychology used in playing video poker.

There is, however, plenty of challenge. The option of holding and discarding cards is a matter of intelligent decision. In general, it's always best to go for the higher hands. Give up a pair if you can go for a one- or two-card draw to an open-end straight or a royal flush.

Look for the machines that pay the highest odds and the biggest progressive jackpots. And again, always play the maximum number of coins to be eligible for the jackpot bonus.

NOTE: Manufacturers of video poker games are offering offshoots, carnival-like games to play that are new wrinkles on poker: Deuces Wild, Double Double Poker, Three-Hand Poker, Five-Hand, Big Split Poker, Ten-Card Stud Poker, Parlay Poker, and Pick'em Poker. Naturally, all these games come onstage just to attract more players, more money, more time with their creations. Remember, before you put a penny in any of these machines, *read them*. Winning hands change, winning returns also change—because with casino games change is always in the air.

5

ROULETTE: LEARNING THE WHEEL AND THE BETTING LAYOUT

Roulette is one of the oldest games in the casino. In fact, it is the most popular of the casino games throughout Europe. Without question it's a game of fun, and with a little knowledge and practice, it can be profitable as well.

Roulette is strictly a game of chance. But, notwithstanding the element of luck involved, there are ways to play the roulette wheel that can enhance your lucky streak and enable you to win progressively larger amounts as your luck continues. In this chapter, we will discuss these methods and betting systems.

The Spinning Wheel

First, let's examine both the wheel and the betting table layout so that you can fully understand all of the bets and procedures in playing roulette.

The roulette wheel is divided into thirty-eight numbered slots, including the numbers 1 through 36 and then a 0 and a 00. In Europe there is only a single 0 and only thirty-seven numbered slots to the wheel. A single-0 wheel can also be found in certain selected casinos in Nevada and Atlantic City.

The house advantage is that with both 0 and 00, the player receives odds payoff of 35:1, rather than the true odds of 37 to 1. That house advantage amounts to 5.6 percent and is how the casinos earn their money. Ostensibly, they make $5.60 on every $100 wagered. The European wheel, with its single 0, has a house advantage of just 2.7 percent; houses there would make $2.70 on every $100 wagered at the roulette table.

In either case, a house rake of 2.7 percent to a fraction over 5 percent is not too bad an edge to combat. By comparison, thoroughbred racetracks take 17 percent to 20 percent for their cut.

All the wheels in Nevada and Atlantic City have the same sequence of numbers spread around the wheel. The table layout is also the same. So, wherever you play, the rules and regulations will be familiar to you.

Getting Acquainted

Roulette is played at a table that seats six to seven players. Each player is assigned a particular colored chip, which remains with that player until he or she leaves the game. Those chips must be cashed in at the roulette table—they do not have value at any other table or at the cashier's cage.

Also, each player may be playing for different stakes. The value of each player's colored chips is set by the player. If a player enters the game by asking for a stack of fifty-cent chips, the dealer will hand over a stack of forty chips, all the same color, and receive $20; for those wishing to play with twenty-five-cent chips, a $20 bill will get them eighty chips. In order to determine the amount of each player's chips, the dealer places one of the colored chips on the rim of the wheel with a price marker on top of that chip. With up to seven players placing bets all over the table, the colored chips quickly identify each player and the dealer makes the proper payoffs quickly and efficiently.

When large amounts are won by the players, the dealer may elect to pay off with regular casino chips of $5 and $25 value. For example, if a player bet two fifty-cent chips on a single number and won, the payoff would be either seventy of the colored chips or $35 in $5 chips. If a player is winning, you'll usually see casino chips and the colored roulette chips stacked up in front of that player.

In diagram 5-1, we see the betting table layout, with the circled letters designating each type of bet that may be made; table 5-I explains each of these bets and their odds payoffs.

Placing Bets

In most casinos, the roulette table has a small sign stating the minimum bet per spin. It's usually a $2 minimum bet: That means $2 in cumulative bets, not one bet for $2. For example, if you're playing with fifty-cent chips, you can put one chip on a single number, another chip on a two-number split bet, and two chips on red. Thus, if your single number or two-number bet loses, but the winning number was red, you'd win two chips on the red bet and lose the other two bets if they didn't hit. In most cases you'll be betting more than four chips, so you'll make the minimum bet qualification.

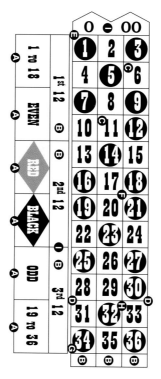

DIAGRAM 5-1

The wheel has exactly eighteen red numbers and eighteen black numbers, with the 0 and 00 colored green. There is only one bad bet on the board: the "E" bet of five numbers—0, 00, 1, 2, 3. In all other bets, whether they're single-number bets, groups, red, black, dozens, columns, etc., the house edge remains at 5.6 percent.

After the player places his bet(s) on the betting layout, the dealer spins the wheel and then rolls the ball in the opposite direction along the top inner edge of the wheel. As the ball slows down it loses force, bounces around the slotted wheel, and finally settles in one of the thirty-eight numbered slots. That number is the declared winner.

Table 5-1

The chips used in roulette are colored for identification only. You set their value when you buy a stack. Using chips or coins, bets are placed on the roulette layout as shown in diagram 5-1. There are red and black numbered squares from number 1 to number 36. These numbers are divided into three groups: first 12, second 12, and third 12. They are also divided for betting purposes into three horizontal groups (see the diagram) from 3 to 36, 2 to 35, and 1 to 34. Bets may also be placed on groups of numbers from 1 to 18, and 19 to 36. Also shown in the diagram are 0 and 00. These are colored green.

Betting may also be made on odd or even numbers or on red and black numbers as the dealer spins the ball. The payoff for roulette bets is as follows (see the diagram for position):

If the ball lands in . . .	
A Red or black or 1-18 or 19-36	even money
B Groups of twelve numbers (dozens)	2:1
A Odd or even	even money
B Groups of twelve numbers (columns)	2:1
C Any one number or 0 or 00	35:1
SPLIT BETS	
D Any one of the six in the group	5:1
E 0, 00, 1, 2, or 3	6:1
F Any one of the four in a group	8:1
G Any one of the three in a group	11:1
H Any one of the two numbers	17:1
I 0 or 00	17:1

The dealer places a marker on that particular number so that all the players can see the results of that spin. The dealer then pays off each player who had a bet on that number or a bet on any related payoff. For example, if the winning number was 17, the following payoffs would be made:

First of all, all bets on the single number 17 would receive thirty-five chips for each chip bet. Number 17 is red, which would give all red bets an even-money payoff. It is also in the 1 to 18 range, and a bet there gets even money. It's in the second dozen, which gives a 2-for-1 payoff, and also in the middle column, and a bet there gets paid off at 2:1. It's an odd-bet win, too.

DIAGRAM 5-2

Betting Blocks

There's another way to select numbers, and for this choice we look at the wheel in diagram 5-2. You will note that the numbers are placed around the wheel not in 1-2-3 order but in another manner. The red 1 is exactly opposite the black 2. The green 00 is opposite the green 0. It continues until we find black 35 opposite red 36.

Many roulette players, especially those who follow systems, play blocks of numbers as seen on the wheel. Here is an example of that method, or system, of betting.

This method requires five chips. Place one chip on a six-number bet, as shown by "D" in diagram 5-1. Let's say you select the block of six numbers 10 through 15. Your one chip would be placed on the line between the 10 and the 13; this signifies a six-number bet covering 10, 11, 12, 13, 14, and 15.

Now take four chips and place one each on 16, 17, 18, and 28. This will give you a total of ten numbers covered with five chips. You'll notice that, as shown in diagram 5-2, your ten numbers are spread around the wheel so that each number is no more than three spaces apart, and in some cases only two numbered slots from each other. When the ball bounces around the wheel, it has a good chance of landing in one of the slots within the numbers you selected.

If one of your six-number group wins, you'll receive five chips to your one-chip bet. Naturally, you will lose the other four chips you bet on the single numbers. But you now have six chips, one more than the five you started with. After such a win, you should now increase your six-number bet to two chips, keeping the same bet of one chip on each of the four single numbers. If you hit one of the four numbers, you'll get a payoff of thirty-five chips, giving you a win of thirty-six chips—less the five chips invested—for a net win of thirty-one chips. When this happens, double all bets. If you are lucky enough to win the third time in a row, double all bets again. This is called *progressive win betting*. Remember: You *never* increase your bets on losses, only on wins.

Take the time to read this chapter over again, so that you can become completely conversant with the game of roulette. Then plan your strategy of betting single numbers and groups so that the next time the wheel spins, you'll be playing roulette for fun as well as profit.

ROULETTE TERMINOLOGY

BLACK—A roulette bet on all the black numbers. Pays 1:1.

BLOCK BETTING—The set of numbers on one section of the wheel, which are bet *en masse* in certain roulette strategies.

COLUMN BET—A bet on an entire column of numbers; there are three available columns. Pays 2:1.

CORNER BET—A roulette four-number bet. Pays 8:1.

COUP—One roll; one decision. Winning bet.

DEALER—The casino employee who conducts the roulette wheel.

DOUBLE-ZERO—A bet on the thiry-eighth number (00) on the wheel, colored green. Pays 35:1, like any other *straight* bet.

DOZENS BET—A bet on any of the three available groups of twelve numbers: 1 through 12, 13 through 24, or 25 through 36. Pays 2:1.

EVEN—A bet on all of the 18 even numbers. Pays 1:1.

GREEN NUMBERS—The zero (0) and double-zero (00).

HIGH or LOW—A bet on either the first eighteen numbers (Low: 1–18) or the second eighteen (High: 19–36). Pays 1:1.

HOUSE PERCENTAGE—The advantage the casino has over the player. In American roulette, it's 5.26 percent.

INSIDE BET—Any bet made on numbers directly inside the layout. Odds for winning inside bets range from 5 to 1, up to 35 to 1.

LINE BET—A bet on any six adjoining numbers. Pays 5:1.

NEIGHBORS—The numbers immediately to the left and right of the winning number.

19–36—A bet on the second half of the numbers in the layout. Pays 1:1.

ODD—A bet on all the odd numbers. Pays 1:1.

1–18—A bet on the first half of the numbers on the wheel. Pays 1:1.

OUTSIDE BET—The betting area on the roulette table bordering the numbers layout. This includes columns, dozens, black/red, odd/even, 1–18, 19–36. Pays 1:1.

PIT BOSS—Supervisor in charge of the roulette wheel.

PROGRESSIVE BETTING—To build up a bet by placing your winnings from the previous bet on top of your current bet.

RED—A roulette bet on all the red numbers. Pays 1:1.

RUN—Series of like results, such as four red or six odd.

SINGLE NUMBER—A roulette straight-up bet. Pays 35:1.

SIX-LINE BET—A roulette six-number bet. Pays 5:1.

SLOTS—Sections of the roulette wheel that hold the numbers.

SPECIAL LINE BET—A bet on the first five numbers: 0, 00, 1, 2 and 3 *only*. Pays 6:1.

SPLIT BET—A bet on any two adjoining numbers. Pays 17:1.

SQUARE/QUARTER BET—A bet on any four numbers in a square. Pays 8:1.

STRAIGHT BET—A bet on any one number. Pays 35:1.

STREET BET—A bet on any three numbers in a line. Pays 11:1.

TOKE—Gratuity or tip for the dealer.

WHEEL CHECKS—The special unmarked chips that are used specifically on roulette tables.

ZERO—A bet on the thirty-seventh number (0) on the wheel; colored green. Pays 35:1, like any other *straight bet*.

KENO: UPPING YOUR CHANCES

As any frequent visitor to Las Vegas knows, one of the most enduring and popular diversions in the Strip hotels and the downtown casinos is the game of keno. Keno is enjoyed for many reasons: It's simple to play, requires no particular skill to win big, and can be played in a leisurely fashion. Whether you're enjoying a sumptuous meal in the hotel restaurant, relaxing in the keno lounge with a cool drink, or standing in the glamorous casino lobby, you'll find the keno numbers are visible from practically anywhere in the hotel. Busy keno writers constantly make the rounds from the restaurant to the keno lounge and through the hotel lobby to dispense winnings and pick up new playing tickets. Simply put, keno is a fascinating game of chance.

The Origins of Keno

Keno today, with its automatic *goose* through which Ping-Pong balls printed with the keno numbers are electrically popped, is not the modern game one might assume it is. Actually, keno dates back to the Chinese Han dynasty, preceding our current version by nearly two thousand years. The game was originally introduced to the public by a man named Cheung Leung, who devised it as a way for the Chinese government to raise much-needed revenues for its army. Originally, 120 different Chinese ideograph characters were used to place bets, but this number was eventually reduced to ninety. The people took to it immediately, making it a smashing success that netted loads of cash for the state. And to this day, keno has enjoyed unflagging popularity.

In the gay nineties, when Chinese immigrants brought the game with them to the United States, the ninety characters were further reduced to eighty. The game soon garnered favor with Americans, who nevertheless found the Chinese ideograph characters hard to differentiate. To facilitate their play, the Chinese characters were replaced by ordinary Arabic numerals from one to eighty. If you pick up a keno ticket today, you will see that it is still numbered from one to eighty.

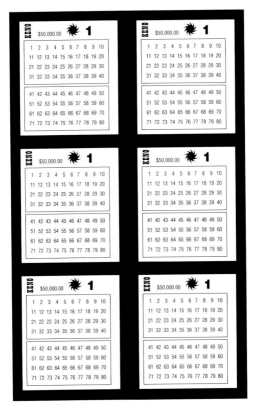

ABOVE: TYPICAL KENO PLAYING CARDS

A few other changes have been made. Originally, wooden balls with the keno numbers on them were pulled by hand through a wooden goose neck. Nowadays, lightweight Ping-Pong balls are used, and they are not manually moved; it's all done by machinery to ensure ease and fairness. The balls are forced aerodynamically through the goose and then pop up, revealing the numbers for that game. The numbers appear on an electrically lighted board in the lobby, the hotel restaurant or, for that matter, almost any place in the casino where one would get the urge to take a chance!

Originally, keno was introduced in Nevada as "racehorse keno," in which each ball popped up bearing not only a number but the name of a racehorse. This "racehorse" aspect was dropped from the game in 1951, when the Nevada government passed a bill taxing off-track betting. So, for the past thirty-one years, it's been strictly a numbers game.

Playing the Game

While sitting in the keno lounge and sipping a drink, you can fill out a paper keno ticket for the low price of seventy cents, using the special black crayon provided, and watch the keno numbers light up on the board over the dealers' station. Although this is not the only locale in the casino where one can play, it's fun to sit in the special keno combination desk chairs (which are a bit like the kind in old schoolhouses, except that they have a convenient compartment for your drink), while cheerful, attractive keno writers are at your beck and call. This is perhaps the only big advantage keno has over the other games in the casino: It can be played in a completely relaxed atmosphere, without the dizzying adrenaline rush that characterizes so many of the table games. This is one of the reasons that keno is such a big favorite with novice bettors and recreational players.

A fascinating aspect of keno is that it is seemingly entirely dependent on chance, with absolutely no way for anybody to predict which numbers will surface in any given game. But there are definitely aspects of the game that you should consider before plunking down your quarters and dimes for a keno ticket. These aspects could very well give you an edge over the average, nonstrategic *straight* keno bettor.

The keno ticket is played by marking off, with circles or X's, anywhere from one to fifteen numbers on a ticket. The payoff on a *straight* bet will be determined by what percentage of your numbers comes up out of the ones that you bet. The minimum price of the keno ticket is usually seventy cents; a higher ticket price, of course, will get you bigger stakes. You give your ticket to the keno writer, for which you'll receive a marked-up duplicate that is stamped with

it's as easy as one-two-three

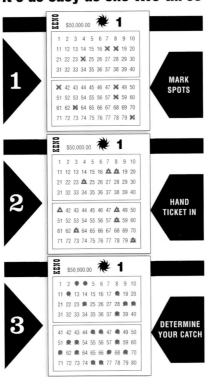

ABOVE: THE STAGES OF A PLAYED KENO CARD

the ticket number, date, and game played. This is your receipt. Then all you do is wait for your numbers to light up!

If you do win a keno game by having a number or numbers light up, you *must* present your ticket to collect your winnings—either to a keno writer or to the dealer directly—before the start of the next game. If you're too tardy in presenting your receipt, your chance to collect will be gone. So, please be prompt.

Betting . . . by the Numbers

If you take the time to scrutinize the payoff sheet, you'll see that the winnings really skyrocket as the proportion of the numbers chosen that come up grows. If you're playing, for example, eight spots for $1.40 and five numbers come up, that nets you a win of $12, which is a payoff of about 8:1. But when you're only playing five numbers, getting all five means you rake in $680—a 485:1 payoff—for the same ticket price!

By looking at these stakes, one might assume that it's best to play few numbers, rather than many, on a *straight* ticket. Is this necessarily so? Well, it all depends on what kind of a player you are. Remember that the house edge in the game of keno is astronomical, probably higher than that of most other games. Some players figure that, taking these high odds into consideration, they might as well play a long-shot game with just a few numbers each time, keeping their fingers crossed and hoping for a miracle. Other bettors play a high or maximum number of spots to increase their chances of having a win, and are content with a much smaller kitty. For example, if the same five spots we mentioned earlier had come up on a ticket on which ten numbers were played for $1.40, the payoff would have been only $2.80—not a killing, certainly, but still enough to play two or three more games and have some fun.

Ways to Play

So far, we've only discussed the *straight* ticket, which, for one price, gives you one shot at one group of numbers. There is, however, a much more sophisticated way of playing keno that, for a slightly higher initial price, gives you a much better shot at picking up some winnings. This is to bet either a *way* or *combination* ticket.

With a way keno bet, your ticket is marked with three or more equal groups of numbers, bringing your ticket price to the number of groups times the amount you're playing; that is, playing three groups of numbers at seventy cents will cost you a total of $2.10. It is a bit more expensive to play this way, so you can't play as many games as you could if you were to just bet seventy-cent straight tickets all night.

But remember, keno is a game that should be played only for short stretches of time anyway, since it's impossible to buck the gigantic house edge over any length of time. And with a way ticket you're much more assured of some kind of shot at a win. If, for example, you mark off three groups of four numbers, you can collect on three eight-spot bets, three four-spot bets, and the total twelve-spot bet, making the ticket price $4.90 but giving you lots of chances to win on just one ticket. Considering all the factors, it's a lot smarter to play this way than to repeatedly take your chances with a one-shot straight ticket. Just make sure that you clearly mark, on the right-hand margin of your keno ticket, the type of bet you're taking.

Now we come to the combination ticket. On this type of bet, you can have groups of numbers of different count—say, two fours and a two—and bet on the different combinations. On a four, four, and two-spot, you might bet on the one two-spot, both four-spots, the two different four-and-two (6) combinations, one eight-spot (the four-and-four), and also play the ticket as a total ten-spot. This gives you a great range of winnings that can come up, again, for a price of $4.90. Remember, too, that this is about the only way of playing that can give you a decent shot at the big stakes.

Compare this type of wager with the more common straight ticket. If you chose twelve spots, for example, on a seventy-cent straight ticket, an eight out of twelve win would net you $150. But the same eight numerals coming up on one eight-spot way or combination ticket will hand you a jackpot of $12,500. The smaller wins are all possible too, of course, but with the odds this high, always think in terms of a big score. Because the keno odds are so hugely in favor of the house, the smart player will use his head and make each ticket really worthwhile.

The Numbers Game

Choosing which numbers to play is a personal, somewhat mystical ritual. It seems remarkable, sometimes, how certain people can invest certain numbers with a strongly directed personal force and almost "will" the numbers to appear. Many people have standard "lucky numbers" that seem to come in for them more often than not. Others will play the number of children that they have, or grandchildren, or the date of Baby's birthday, or perhaps an anniversary number.

Some canny players watch the games for a few hours without placing any bets, and write down the numbers that seem to recur frequently. There are two schools of thought on how to handle these commonly seen numbers. One method is to favor these particular numbers when making your bets, since if they've been coming up regularly there's no real reason they should stop. Perhaps there is a physical reason for this, as well: These common-show numbers may appear often because the balls holding the other numbers are scratched or damaged in some way, and aren't as likely to pop up into the goose. (But, then again, there is the theory that one should definitely play the numerals that haven't been seen in quite a while, since, according to the law of averages, they're "due" to make a showing.)

To summarize, then, the best method of playing keno is to opt for the way or combination tickets, using a pool of numbers drawn from your own personal favorites, the ones commonly seen that day, and perhaps one or two digits you haven't seen in a while. Then order a drink, relax, and get ready to win!

KENO TERMINOLOGY

COMBINATION TICKET—A keno ticket on which several groups of numbers are played.

GOOSE—The clear-plastic apparatus through which modern keno balls are aerodynamically propelled. In the past, the goose was made of wood.

KENO WRITERS—The people who comb the casino, collecting keno tickets and delivering winnings. The same term applies to those who write tickets behind the counter.

KING TICKET—A keno ticket on which one (king) number is used to pair up with groups of numbers.

RACE-HORSE KENO—A previously played form of keno in which each ball was imprinted with the name of a racehorse as well as a number.

STRAIGHT TICKET—A keno ticket that is played as one set of numbers.

WAY TICKET—The same as a combination ticket.

7

POKER: THE PEOPLE'S CHOICE

Poker has been, and continues to be, one of the most popular of all the social card games. Although we have other popular card games, such as bridge (which is played widely across the nation, and even abroad), gin rummy, hearts, and pinochle, poker continues to be the best kind of gambling card game.

It's estimated that there are over 40 million serious-minded poker players throughout the United States. These are people who play regularly in a weekly game, usually with the same friendly group. They play at home, in social and country clubs, or in the various business service organizations.

Mapping It Out

Poker is very popular throughout every jurisdiction where Class II and Class III gaming is legal. There are card rooms all over California, and poker rooms are found in almost all Indian and off-reservation casinos in the States.

And all the styles or versions of the game are played. Stakes go anywhere from as small as $1 to $3 bets, up to $15 and $30, $50, and $100, and, in some places, no-limit stakes where pots may reach as high as $100,000.

What's the Deal?

There are many different kinds of poker games. We will deal, however, with the card games played in the states mentioned.

Stud poker is the game in which one gets two or three cards dealt face down, then four cards dealt up, for a six- or seven-card game. Five-card stud is where four cards are dealt up with one card down (in the hole). Then there is the popular game of seven-card stud, where there are four cards open and three down cards in your hand. There's also high-low draw, and high-low stud, which gives a win to both the high hand and the low hand.

Then there is the boss game, Texas Hold'em, in which the lowest hand wins. A straight of ace, 2, 3, 4, 5 is the lowest hand. Ace counts for one, and the second lowest hand is ace, 2, 3, 4, 6, then ace, 2, 3, 5, 6, and so on.

These are the most popular games played in the various

card rooms and poker clubs around the country. Now here are explanations of each game, starting with draw poker.

Draw Poker

The first requirement of the game is to *ante,* which means that a previously agreed-upon amount of money is placed on the table by each player. This serves the dual purpose of giving each player an incentive to win and at the same time helps to eliminate the problem of the proverbial quitter who always folds unless he instantly draws four to a royal flush.

Next, five cards are dealt face down to each player and it is time to determine who is going to open the betting and then who is going to *call* (match) the bet or raise it. The general rule is that it takes a pair of jacks or better to open. This is when you have to exercise caution and have the necessary knowledge to make an accurate analysis of the odds. The odds depend upon how many players are involved, where you are sitting, and who opens before you. Speaking in very general terms, the odds are quite high that everyone is going to be dealt at least one pair. If you happen to have a pair of jacks, the probability that someone else has a pair of queens or kings is very high. Out of the heart of Texas comes a quote that is extremely appropriate here: "I don't open with jacks. That's gambling, and my Daddy taught me never to gamble."

Pay close attention to the odds. It would be an excellent idea to pick up one of the many available books on analyzing the odds and study it until you can commit most of it to memory. If you are capable of accurately understanding the odds, you will be way ahead of the opponent who goes on hunches and gut-level feelings. His "feelings" will probably end up putting money in your pockets.

The easiest rule of thumb would be that if you are sitting directly to the left of the deal, then open with aces. If you are two seats or more from the dealer, open with nothing lower than kings. If someone in the seventh seat opens first, figure that he has at least a pair of jacks, and don't stay in the game unless you have at least a pair of queens. If you plan to raise the opening bet, be sure that you can beat any pair. The rules on betting vary from game to game and go all the way from unlimited betting to the more common system of having a fixed amount and/or a fixed number of raises.

Now, all the betting for this round has come to a halt and you are ready to draw. Again, there are variations on the theme. You can "rebuild" your hand by discarding from one to five cards (the latter amount only if allowed) and getting new ones in exchange. If you have a *pat* hand, you are satisfied with the original cards dealt to you in the first place. Again, there are odds to consider and, as mentioned earlier, if there is $10 in the pot and you're betting $2, then your return, if you win, will be 5:1. What you must consider is that if your cards indicate that the odds are 22 to 1 that you won't win, then you should not be staying in the game, because the odds of winning should be better than the pot odds.

Once you know your odds and, based on the laws of probability, it appears that you have the winning hand, go for it, all the way! If you're running scared about losing your shirt, you shouldn't be in the game in the first place. Part of the battle is to come to the table armed with the proper knowledge; the other part is to back yourself up financially, without any doubts, once you're ready to make your move.

One final note: It's best not to play poker with people you've never met before. It's hard enough to "read" the expressions of people you know, let alone to come out ahead with a bunch of total strangers.

Five-Card Stud

Unlike draw poker, there is only one hidden card in this game—the first one, which is dealt face down. Before the betting, one more card is dealt face up. Then after each round of betting another card is dealt until you have five.

In this game, the main thing to look for is a pair of *anything.* A pair of twos can easily take you straight to the bank because of the limited amount of cards dealt in this game.

One of the ways to psych out your opponents is to notice if

anyone keeps checking his down card. It couldn't be all that great if he can't even remember what it is!

Now, if you're hoping to pick up the fourth and/or fifth card to a straight or a flush, you're treading in deep water. The only time you would stay in under these circumstances would be if no one is betting, in which case you can *check,* meaning you get a free ride this time around. In this game, if you're being stared in the face by an ace in someone else's hand, look around for other aces. If one or two others are exposed also, the chances are slim to none that anyone will get their pair.

If you've definitely got the only game in town, play somewhat cautiously. You don't want to scare everyone off by your overly bold betting. Keep everyone interested, if you can, and then grab the money and run.

Seven-Card Stud

Two more cards and what do you get? Seven-card stud, a most interesting game that is full of unexpected variables. Part of the intrigue is that the first two cards and the last card are dealt face down and the other four are exposed. Also, the pot gets bigger because there is an extra round of betting.

With two cards down, it is a lot more difficult to figure out what's going on in your opponents' hands. Also, there are many schools of thought on how to play this game. Some people arbitrarily stay in to get their fourth card before they decide whether to fold or not. A lot of good players stay in only if they have a pair concealed or perhaps a split pair, or, of course, anything better.

The best clue to look for is this: If you are beaten on sight after four cards are dealt, it's a good time to fold your hand. Please be forewarned, though, that to stay in on a hunch or a hope is usually a losing proposition.

One rule of thumb is to pay close attention to the big bettors who *appear* to have "nothing much" going for them. It's very easy to get deceived in this game, so if you don't have the cards to play and you stay . . . you'll pay!

High-Low Draw

If you already know how to play draw poker, then the only change now is that the pot will be split between the high and the low hands. The amateur player has a tendency to shy away from going for a high hand. Holding out for a low hand can be terribly disappointing when a one-eyed jack is staring you right in the face, especially after you have just bet your life savings during the last three betting rounds. There are two major variations: one where the players declare whether they are going for high or low or both, the other where "cards speak."

High-Low Seven-Card Stud

This game has an interesting twist . . . you can go either high or low and, in some cases, both high and low. Since you have seven cards to rearrange any way you want, you can often set up a good low hand and then find out you have the winning high straight as well. According to one set of rules, if you are going both high and low (often known as going *pig*) and someone else has you beat for either high or low, you are completely out of the game.

Lowball

As the name implies, it is the lowest hand that wins this game. However, the rules vary on how to arrive at the winning hand. According to one set of official rules, aces are low; so therefore a pair of aces is lower than a pair of deuces. Also, straights don't count, so the perfect low would be ace through 5 (often referred to as a *bicycle*). On the other hand, there is another way to play it with straights being high and, therefore, the perfect low would be ace, 2, 3, 4, and 6 . . . and still a third way, called *razz,* where the ace is high, as are straights and flushes, and the lowest hand is 2, 3 ,4, 5, 7.

Poker Games with a Wrinkle

Some casino executives call the following "table games" carnival games. Others fancy the name "exotic games." They are Caribbean Stud, Let It Ride, Three-Card Poker, and Pai Gow.

Caribbean Stud

This is a five-card stud game, and it's played on a blackjack table sporting a new felt cover with graphics on its surface. These graphics indicate where the player places his chips, or bets.

The standard fifty-two-card deck is used and, when the game gets rolling, the cards come out of a multideck shoe, or from an automatic shuffler dealing five-card hands at a time.

Simply put, players try to beat the dealer.

Each player's area of the table has three marked spots: One is a bet spot, the second is marked ante, and the third is a slot with blinking lights, usually red.

Before the cards are dealt, the player places a bet on the ante spot. The amount can be the casino minimum or larger, within house limits.

The player also has the option of taking a shot at a progressive jackpot, which is a part of all Caribbean Stud games. Players insert a dollar into the progressive jackpot slot—and are now ready to play Caribbean Stud.

Players receive five cards, all face down. The dealer gets four cards face down, and one face up.

Now then, you, as a player, look at your cards, check the one card the dealer has up, and decide to either stick and stay or fold and go away.

If you feel your five-card hand is worthless, you fold and lose your ante bet. If you decide to stay and play, you place a bet in the bet spot on the table.

This bet must be twice the amount of your ante bet. OK? That done, you and the dealer turn over your hands; if you beat the dealer's hand, you win.

Now know this: In Caribbean Stud, the dealer has to qualify with an ace, king, or higher to play. If the dealer does not have ace, king, or better, then the game stops—and the house pays the player even money, one for one, on the ante bet. On the call bets, it's considered a push. And your dollar in the progressive jackpot slot is a contribution to the growing jackpot.

If the dealer's hand beats your hand, you lose both bets. If you beat the dealer, you get even money on a pair or less, 2:1 on two pair, 3:1 on three of a kind, and the following payoffs on these hands:

straight: 4:1

flush: 5:1

full house: 7:1

four of a kind: 20:1

straight flush: 50:1

royal flush: 100:1

Now, if you placed the dollar in the jackpot slot you also receive a bonus:

An extra $50 for a flush.

An extra $100 for a full house.

And an extra $500 for four of a kind.

If you hit a straight flush, you win 10 percent of the total jackpot.

If you land a royal flush, you win 100 percent of the total jackpot.

Let It Ride

Here's a poker game where you, as a player, do not play against other players, nor do you play against the dealer—in fact, the dealer works with you toward building a winning hand.

Here's the deal on Let It Ride: It is played using a standard fifty-two-card deck. It is played on a blackjack table covered with new felt. On the felt, in front of each player's betting area, are three circles. One circle is marked One (1), another Two (2), and the third has a dollar sign ($) inside it.

The dollar-sign circle is the one bet that always stays in play.

First things first: Players must get a pair of tens or better to be eligible to win.

Before the deal, each player places three equal bets in each circle. The bets can be the house minimum; in this case, let's say $3, meaning each circle has $3 for a total bet—so far—of $9.

There is also a circle on the board where each player can place an additional dollar in order to be in on a bonus payoff should the gods of cards be kind.

The dealer now doles out three cards, face down, to each player.

That completed, the dealer places two cards face down in the spots marked for those two cards.

You, as a player, look at your three cards. You're discerning if the three cards are worthy of a bet—the bet being the $3 in the first circle.

If not, you pull back the money on the first circle.

Now you've got $6 invested. But you're still in the game.

The dealer now turns over one of the two "house" cards.

Does it help? Did you catch a pair?

You see if that card can help you, and if you like what you see, you tell the dealer to let it ride. The dealer now turns over the second card and you turn over your three cards.

If your five cards—the three you were dealt, and the two the dealer had—come to have tens or better, and the dealer cannot beat your hand, you win all the bets you've let ride. (See the following table for your payoff numbers.)

Sadly, if you were not able to beat the dealer, you lose the bet in the dollar-sign circle and all bets left in the two numbered circles.

An item to remember: You can pull back your second bet even if you allowed your first bet to ride.

LET IT RIDE PAYOUT TABLE

pair, tens or better: 1:1

two pair: 2:1

three of a kind: 3:1

straight: 5:1

flush: 8:1

full house: 11:1

four of a kind: 50:1

straight flush: 200:1

royal flush: 1,000:1

BONUS PAYOUT TABLE
straight: $20
flush: $50
full house: $75
four of a kind: $200
straight flush: $2,000
royal straight flush: $10,000

The Wild and Wooly World of Three-Card Poker

First, three-card poker is a game of many names. It wears several outfits, but underneath, in its nakedness, it's still a three-card poker game.

The standard fifty-two-card deck is used. Players go only against the dealer, the house. There are three bets to make, the first being an ante bet, which is the house minimum, and is mandatory—if you wish to participate. The second wager is titled *play*. The third is a bonus bet called *pair plus*.

The game starts when players place their ante bets; each player is then dealt three cards, as is the dealer.

The player then looks at the three cards that were dealt. If the player does not like the cards, he folds—losing the ante wager. If the player likes the three cards, a bet at least equal to the ante is made in the "play" box.

When those bets are in place, everyone turns over their cards. Now, here's the first order of business in three-card poker to see who wins what.

The dealer, in order to qualify, has to have at least a queen high. If the dealer doesn't qualify, all active players get even money on their ante bets—they push on the play bets. The exception here is, any player having a straight or better gets paid an additional ante bonus shown below.

If the dealer does qualify, those who can't beat him lose ante and play bets, but they can still win if they have a straight or higher.

Those happy players who do beat the dealer get even money

on their ante and play bets.

The *pair plus* bet is the bonus bet, which is usually the house minimum and is made before the cards are dealt. As mentioned, the play bet is not made unless the player wants to go on after seeing the three cards dealt.

THREE-CARD POKER PAY TABLE:

Play bets, at least, must always equal ante bets
Dealer plays with queens or better

When dealer does not play: play bets push; ante bets pay 1:1
When dealer does play: play bets pay 1:1; ante bets pay 1:1

Ante bonus pays	**Pair plus pays**
straight: 1:1	pair: 1:1
three of a kind: 4:1	flush: 3:1
straight flush: 6:1	straight: 6:1
	three of a kind: 30:1
	straight flush: 40:1

Note on three-card poker: The reason a straight is paid higher than a flush is simply that it's harder to catch a straight in three cards than it is to come up with a flush.

East Meets West in Pai Gow

A long, long time ago in China, a game known as Pai Gow was played with special dice and dominoes. It was designed to be a slow game . . . a s-l-o-w game. Players wanted to spend hours, more in one another's company than in the actual play by play of the game.

My, how times have changed. Today's Pai Gow, though still leisurely compared with craps or video slots, is quick enough to satisfy most any casino visitor in search of games with a new wrinkle.

Pai Gow is played with a standard fifty-two-card deck, plus a joker, for a total of fifty-three cards. The game is played on a blackjack table covered with felt and dotted with graphics in front of each gamer's playing area.

Player's receive seven cards, face down. The goal is to make two hands out of those seven cards—a *low*, or *front* hand using only two cards.

Using the other five cards the player makes a *high*, or *back* hand.

Your front—the two-card hand—should never be stronger than the back hand. If that happens, it's a *foul* and you lose both hands.

The five-card hand is ranked in strength just as it is in regular poker, except that an ace through 5 straight is the second highest

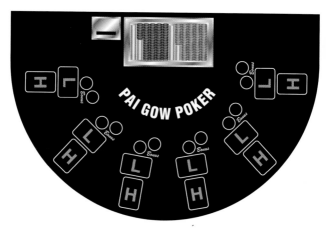

DIAGRAM 5-2

hand in Pai Gow, stronger than a 9 through king. The front hand (two cards) is high singles, or a pair, with a pair of aces rated the highest.

Betting is as simple as it gets: You bet before the first card is dealt. And that's the end of it. Some casinos call for separate bets on front and back hands, but this is rather unusual.

The game is on: The dealer gives you seven cards, the dealer receives seven cards . . . you build your front and back hands. The dealer does likewise.

Then the dealer turns over all the cards and starts comparing:

If both your hands are weaker than the dealer's, you lose front and back. If both your hands beat the dealer's, you win both. If you win one and lose one, it's a push. And if your hand and the dealer's hand match, it's called *copies* and the dealer wins. Winners collect on a 1 to 1 ratio.

Now then, there is a little more: The dealer is also the banker. In Pai Gow, you as a player can also be the banker. You have that opportunity, with the proviso that you have the bankroll to handle all payoffs.

Finally, all winning hands are assessed a 5 percent commission—you as a player and you as the banker.

For the mathematically inclined, the house has about a 2.5 percent advantage in Pai Gow.

Note: Some casinos offer a bonus feature to the game. Check to see if the one you're in has that attraction.

Texas Hold'em

It's the hottest casino live poker game in America today. The televising of the World Series of Poker from Binion's Horseshoe (now Harrah's) in Las Vegas certainly helped. The game is basically a seven-card stud game with a few twists that make it intriguing enough to keep everyone on the edge of their seats. This game definitely could be subtitled "Kill or Be Killed."

Here's the game: Two players to the left of the dealer put up the initial bets; they foot the bill for the rest of the players. But this responsibility moves around the table after each hand. So, as the game progresses, all players take turns being the *small* and *big blinds*. The first player is called the small blind; he starts by putting up, say $2; the next player is called the big blind, and puts up twice what the small blind put up. So he's in for $4. Two cards are now dealt to each player, face down.

Now comes the first round of betting: Options are to fold, bet, or raise. Only one bet and three raises are allowed per player, on the first round. And players cannot check on the first round, as those blinds are considered bets, not antes. Next, three communal cards are dealt face up—this action is called the *flop*. These three cards belong to all the players and can be used in concert with the two hole cards in the player's hands. This now brings about the second round of betting. Options are to check, bet, fold, or raise. Now comes the fourth communal card, face up—this one is called the *turn*.

And the third round of betting gets under way. Options, again, are to check, fold, bet, or raise. Now, then, if there are at least two players in the game, the fifth and final communal card is dealt, face up, and is called the *river*.

Time for the final round of betting—it's showdown time. All remaining players create the best five-card hand possible, using the player's two pocket, or hole cards, and the five communal cards. Best hand wins. If two hands tie, they split the pot.

Omaha Hi/Lo—The Game for Thinkers

Omaha Hi/Lo is a poker game for thinkers. The game's a challenge to even the most experienced of players. If you snooze, you'll lose.

Much like Texas Hold'em, the deal, called the *button*, moves around the table even though the casino dealer never moves but remains seated at the center, facing the fan of players around him.

To start, the first two players to the dealer's left are called the small blind and the big blind. The small blind starts by placing half of the *structured bet* in front of him or her. "Structured" is used to describe the dollar size of the game: A structured $2 to $4 game of Limit Omaha Hi/Lo would call for the small blind to put up $1, followed by the big blind coming in with a full structured bet of $2.

That done, the dealer gives each player four hole cards, face down. Then the first round of betting begins with the player immediately to the left of big blind. What the player is doing is matching the bet of the small blind ($1), or possibly raising to the bet of the big blind ($2), or perhaps raising the bet to the total of both of the blind's bets: $3. Betting continues around the table back to the blinds.

Next, the dealer places three communal cards in the center of the table, face up. This is called the *flop*. Along with the four "hole" cards, the player has in his hands, the three flop cards now become part of the hand.

Round two of betting begins. Players can bet, raise, or fold. Only the first player can check. Once a bet is made, check time is over.

After the second round of betting is complete, the dealer places one card in the center of the table, face up. This act is called the *turn*.

There are now four up-cards on the table, and each player still in the game has four hole cards.

Round three of betting gets under way—bet, raise, or fold.

Finally comes the fifth up-card, known as the *river*. And now comes the final round of betting—and remember now, we are playing Hi/Lo.

In Omaha Hi/Lo you use *two* cards from your hole cards, the cards in your hand. You can use only *two hole cards,* and any three communal cards, to make the *highest* five-card hand. Conversely, you can use only *two hole cards* to make the *lowest* five-card hand, using three low communal cards to help you get a piece of the pie (pot).

It's a game to ponder. It's two games in one; a low hand can get blown out of the water by the river card. Or it can be a lifesaver for a high hand.

POKER TERMINOLOGY

ANTE—To place an agreed-upon amount of money on the table before the draw. Each player bets the same amount.

BLUFF—The ability to misrepresent one's hand.

CALL—To match the previous bet.

CHECK—When the player passes on his turn.

DRAW—The basic style of poker in which each player is dealt five cards, face down, jacks or better to open.

FIVE-CARD STUD—The type of poker in which only the first card is dealt face down and the other four are face up.

FLUSH—Any five cards, all of the same suit.

FOLD—What a player does when he tosses his cards face down, thus eliminating himself from that hand. When the player folds, he forfeits any ante or previous bets.

FOUR OF A KIND—Any four cards of the same denomination, i.e., four queens, four 9s, etc.

FULL HOUSE—A hand with three of a kind and two of a kind, of any denomination.

HIGH-LOW DRAW—Draw poker, in which the pot is split between the highest and the lowest hands.

HIGH-LOW STUD—A version of poker played with seven cards, in which each player can wager an arrangement of cards as being either the highest or the lowest—or playing both (called *playing pig*) a high and low arrangement.

HOLD'EM—A variation of seven-card poker in which five common cards are shared by the players and two cards more are held by each player individually.

JOKER—A card used as a wild card. In California poker clubs, the joker may be used for aces, straights, and flushes only.

LOWBALL—A version of poker in which the low hand wins.

PAIR—Two of a kind.

PASS—To *not* bet.

POT—The total number of chips bet in the hand from the first bet to the final bet.

RAISE—To increase the previous bet.

ROYAL FLUSH—The 10, jack, queen, king, and ace of one suit. This is poker's top hand.

SEVEN-CARD STUD—Seven-card poker, in which the first two and the last card are dealt face down and the other four are exposed.

STRAIGHT FLUSH—Five cards of the same suit in sequence.

TRIPS—Three of a kind.

WILD CARD—A card that can be used in place of any other card in the deck. This card is predetermined by house rules.

MONEY MANAGEMENT: A METHOD FOR WINNING MORE AND LOSING LESS

Money management is definitely an integral part of casino gaming. Whichever table games you're playing (craps, blackjack, baccarat, roulette), it is necessary to do two things: limit your losses and magnify your wins. This objective can be accomplished through proper money management. It's a simple thing to come by, and in this chapter we're going to tell you about money management and how it can help you to win more money and limit your losses, giving you a much nicer vacation wherever you may go for gaming fun and excitement.

Self-Control Is the Key

To start with, the term "money management" has to do with the control of your bets so that, on one hand, you reduce the loss risk to a stipulated amount, but on the winning side, there are no restrictions. Yes, it's the perfect method of betting. It can account for winning more money when your luck is good, when the dice are rolling well, when blackjack is hitting . . . whatever the game may be. On the other hand, when you're not winning, you will learn through money management how to conserve your bankroll.

Money management, in a word, is a form of *discipline.* Your money management starts to work almost immediately upon your arrival at the gaming site. As soon as you walk into the hotel, it's a matter of not rushing to put a dollar in a slot machine, $5 on the craps table, $1 on the spin of a roulette wheel . . . or whatever the amount, or whatever the game. The idea in money management is that you *plan* your forays into the various table games. All of this, incidentally, simply adds to the pleasure, fun, and excitement of your favorite game, as well as your winning potential. So, the first thing you do upon checking into the hotel is divide your bankroll into certain amounts. For example, let's say that you are there for a two-day stay, and during your stay you're obviously going to play at the tables, dine, see some shows, and enjoy various forms of entertainment. The difference between winning and losing money is sometimes definitely affected by how well you're enjoying your holiday.

A Betting Exercise

Let's say you're playing with $400 over a period of two days. You're going to divide that $400 into four sessions on one day and four sessions on another day. Four hundred is divided into eight equal parts to start; if you win money, things can change, as you will see. So you wind up with $50 per session. A session means you take that $50, walk over to the craps (or roulette, etc.) table, and that is the money you're going to gamble with during that playing session. The playing session ends when you walk away from the table, having lost that $50. If, on the other hand, you walk away with chips to cash in, that also ends that playing session.

Now you go to the table, hand the dealer $50 at a $5 minimum table, and get ten $5 chips back for your cash. If you refer back to our section on how to play winning craps, you'll know how to do what we suggested. But let's say you put $5 on the line, the shooter rolls a point, and you play $5 back on the line because you want to get your full odds, and after a few rolls you've lost $10. The next shooter comes up and, in many cases, people will start to double up at this point, figuring, "Well, I lost the last time, so I'm gonna try ten dollars this time, and see if I can recoup my lost money." That would be the wrong thing to do. In money management—and this is one of the strictest rules—you *never* double up on a previous loss. You do not increase your bet in any way on a previous loss.

So, according to our procedure, you place another $5 bet, and if again the shooter rolls a 4, you've got $5 in back of the line. Remember, when you're betting the line, you always take the odds in back, because that brings the percentage way down. Your pass line bets always pay even money. Your odds bets, which can be the equivalent of the amount of money on the pass line, can give you higher odds and bigger winnings.

Lo and behold, let's say the shooter rolls another 7 and you've lost. You're now $20 out. Again, you are faced with the temptation of doubling up to win. But that's not how it works. There's no such thing as hunches, lucky feelings, etc.; they just don't work at the craps table.

Again, after your second loss, you put $5 on the line. Now the shooter rolls, up comes a 7, and you win $5. This is your first win, and according to our procedure, we always double the amount of the bet on our first win. So this time, after the dealer pays you $5, you double up and $10 goes on the line. The next roll produces an 11, and you win again. Now you've got another $10 that you're paid off, so you've got $20. Our rule calls for taking one chip back—$5. (We always use the term *unit*: betting one unit—and when you win, you bet two units.) In this case our unit has been $5, but it could be $25 as well.

Now you have three units riding on the line.

* * *

Now the shooter comes out with a 6 for a number. As we mentioned, you should always take the odds in back of your bet. So, you take $15 and put it in back of your $15 line bet. The roller rolls a couple of more times and then makes the 6. You now get paid $15 on the line, which gives you six units there, and for your $15 odds bet, which was in back of your $15 line bet you get paid $18—six dollars for each five. So now you pick up the $18, together with your $15 odds bet, but you let the $30 ride on the pass line because of the method of doubling up called "progressive betting," as we will show you after we finish this section You bet one, win; bet two, win; take one down and bet three. Now, when you make your three bet, you have six, and leave the six to ride. This is important because this is your biggest bet so far. The shooter comes out and shoots a 7. He makes a natural 7, and you've just won another $30 (or six units). Now, the rule tells us that we bet four units and take down two units in net profits. So, out of your $60 you now have $60 going, you've won $30, and have twelve $5 units. So you're taking $40 back (eight units) and letting four units ride. Your net profit off your line bets is now $40. In addition to the $18 won previously, you're now $58 ahead, minus the $20 loss, so you're actually $38 ahead.

Now let's say the shooter rolls a 9. You've got a $20 pass line bet, you take $20 and put it in back of your $20 line bet. The shooter rolls a few more numbers and then he comes back with a 9. You get paid $20 on the line, giving you nine units or $40, and you get 30 for 20 on your odds bet, so you get $30 there, and you put this in your rack along with your $20 odds bet.

So, you're off to a good score, which continues like this. Any time you win on one unit, you bet two. Take your four units and take one down, betting three. Three units win on the line, you have six, you bet, you win and you have twelve, you take down eight, you have four going.

* * *

Now, the reason for this method of betting, instead of doubling up on top of the other, is that we do not know, in a chance game like craps or roulette, if the next throw of the dice or turn of the wheel will give us a winner or a loser. So if we hit on a "lucky streak," like the last hand, we don't know if it will continue. Never count on a lucky streak continuing, because you never can tell just when it will end. Every time another win comes, sure, it adds to the lucky streak. But you must always talk about a streak like this in retrospect, not trying to project it into the future, because we cannot predict the future. So, make the most of your wins, but use common sense. Leave enough on to take advantage of another win if you're lucky, but take something back in the event that you lose, so you still have some safe profits from the previous wins.

Let's say that on the next roll the shooter rolls a crap, ace-deuce. This is a loss, so you take back five units and play the original one unit, $5. Once you get a loss, you cannot make the same size bet or add anything. If you're wiped out on your pass line bet, you start all over with one unit. Same method: If that wins, you bet two; if that wins, you bet three; if that wins, you bet six; bet wins, you bet four; wins, bet five. You just keep repeating that form.

In this way, you are minimizing the amount you can lose and maximizing your wins while safeguarding them at the same time.

So here you are, back to your single $5 one-unit bet. Now the roller shoots an 8, and you take $5 and put it in back of the 8, and the shooter rolls a 7, so you've lost the $5 line bet and the

$5 odds in back; so when the next shooter comes up you put $5 on the line again. But you will see that if you count up, you're still ahead this way in spite of a few losses, because you have used this progressive betting system.

Remember: The formula is, bet one, win; bet two, win; bet three, win; bet six, win; bet four and take back eight. (See table 8-1.) Conversely, if you had taken the $50 and lost it all, you would walk away knowing you have three other $50 playing sessions.

The Progressive Money Management System
Bet in Units

A unit should be a one-chip denomination, such as $1, $5, $25. Conceivably, though, if you wanted your unit bets to be larger than $1 but not as much as $5, your unit bet could be $2 (two $1 chips). For the purpose of the chart, we're going to use $5 chips as our units, as we did in the previous example.

This time we will play our progressive money management method at the roulette table. Here you have a choice of betting even-money situations and also areas in which you receive 2:1 for a winning wager. Each spin of the wheel gives you a win or lose decision. (You may wish to review Chapter 5 to refresh your memory of the roulette rules and table layout.)

* * *

According to the odds of roulette as it is played in the casinos of Nevada and Atlantic City, there are thirty-eight selections around the wheel in which to bet. They are the numbers 1 through 36, 0, and 00. The true probability of selecting one of these numbers is 1 in 38, or odds of 37 to 1. However, the casino needs a little edge and it pays 35:1. You put a $1 chip on a number and if it comes up on that spin of the wheel, you get 35:1, or a total of $36. That gives the house a 5¼ percent edge, which is not the worst bet in the world; you pay 17 percent at the thoroughbred racetracks.

If you were to make ten thousand $1 bets on an even-money bet such as red or black, and if the wheel showed an equal number of red as black, you'd lose $525 at the end of the ten thousand spins. The green 0 and 00 is the house edge, and they would show up just enough for you to lose 5¼ percent of your bankroll.

Of course, it's not likely that you'd see *exactly* 525 green numbers during any designated ten thousand roulette spins. But the house edge is a reality, and making flat bets (all the same denomination) will eventually whittle your bankroll down to nothing.

Therefore, if you are to win, you must bet progressively. Table 8-1, which follows, further explains and illustrates our progressive money management system. The betting formula is l-2-3*-6-4**-8. (Bets are $5 units.)

TABLE 8-1			
Units bet	Win	Lose	Cumulative Won-Loss
1	1		+1
2		2	−1
start over 1		1	−2
start over 1	1		−1
2	2		+1
*take 1 unit back 3	3		+4
let 6 ride 6	6		+10
**take 8, let 4 ride 4		4	+6
start over; next bet is 1			

You advance your bets, making them progressively larger, when you win. But always go back to the original one-unit bet when a loss occurs. The idea of taking some profits off during the win sequence is one that ensures that you will show some net profit on any win sequence. You continue to progressively advance your bets with each previous win.

The two-unit win bet gives you four units. However, you drag one unit, which was your original starting bet. You play the three units, and if it wins, let it ride. Then, when that wins, you take off eight units in profit, letting four units ride. The next bet would be the full eight units, and with a win there, you can move up to a ten-unit bet, dragging six units in profit.

In other words, if a really hot hand is unfolding, you want to be on it with progressively higher bets, yet taking profits along the way.

Put Some Aside

When do you know if it's time to leave the craps table? Here is the rule: As soon as you have accumulated double your bankroll, put your original bankroll (say it's $50) off to one side of your chip rack, *where it's not to be touched again!* Now you're playing with the $50 in profits. You're using the money management plan that helped you win the $50 in the first place.

Suppose you get lucky and win another $50 with your $50 profits. You take another $50 and put it aside, as you did with your original bankroll. This is just like putting it in your pocket. Each time you win another $50, you put it on the side or in your pocket to take with you. There is no way you can lose that money once it's been put aside. If you ever lose the money that's in front of you, do not dip into your previous winnings to attempt to recoup. Leave that money alone once it's been put aside.

This philosophy tells us that as long as we continue to win back our original bankroll, we can continue to play in this session. This way, you can combine the thrill of winning with the security of knowing that you won't walk away from the table a loser no matter what happens in your subsequent wagering. Most players don't have a method or formula like this to guide them. When they do win, they're good candidates for losing it all. This can't happen to you as long as you stick to this formula, because the temptation to pile chips on a winning bet without restraint is counteracted. In games of chance, remember that our "winning streak" or lucky cycle is only as good as the last win.

The beautiful part of this method of progressive betting is that for as long as you can gather those increments of $50 each time and put $50 in your pocket, you can continue to play in that session.

Once you get far enough ahead, you might want to take the risk of doubling up a whole roll, because you're only risking profits—some of them, not all. So whether you win or lose big on that particular roll, remember that you're still ahead of the game and you're protecting yourself.

Remember the Guidelines

Your goal is to keep building those $50 increments, and whenever you can do that, keep playing that session. Incidentally, you can always trade in $5 chips for $25 chips, or "green chips," to save space in your pocket or on your rack. You leave the table when you lose the playing money in front of you. You *never* dip back into your previous wins in your pocket or on the side of your rack to take out money once you've lost the amount in your current play. This way, you can walk away from the table a winner even if you've just lost all the money in your playing increment. You hope this won't happen, of course, but the idea is that even if it does, you can still walk away with the feeling of being "home free."

Once you're playing, the progressive system is working out beautifully, and you're beginning to amass some impressive winnings, you can switch from $5 units to $25 units. In that case, you've got to go in with about $200, eight $25 chips, but *the same rules apply.* You're just moving up in the world! Using these principles, you can go from winning hundreds to winning thousands. But it's worth repeating: *Stick to the principles set forth here. Never* increase your bets on a previous loss. *Always* increase your bets on a previous win (only with winning chips that the dealer has paid you). The same principles work for the Wheel of Fortune, baccarat, or any game of chance. Don't forget to use these principles in all eight playing sessions.

Remember that this philosophy—as well as your own discipline in adhering to it—will serve you well in any game of chance, at any betting level. Good luck, and win big!

GAMING TOURNAMENTS: LEARNING
THE RULES AND REQUIREMENTS

Casino-sponsored gaming tournaments are relatively new on the gambling scene, whether they're in Vegas, Reno, Tahoe, or Atlantic City. For the longest time, visitors came to these resorts mainly to play the usual casino games. But now the hotels have a lot of competition with each other, and must tempt visitors with something new. Thus, tournaments came into being.

Poker Tournaments

Actually, for the past ten years there *have* been poker tournaments, the most notable being the World Series of Poker sponsored by Binion's Horseshoe Casino in downtown Las Vegas. Today this is a million-dollar tournament in which all kinds of poker games are played over a period of about four weeks. They start off with smaller pots like $25 to $100,000, moving all the way up to a $1 million game. This has brought in many crack poker players from all over the country, because the contestants get a good break when they enter the tournaments. It's very festive, attracts a lot of spectators, and the sponsoring hotel is giving something to the tournaments. For example, in Binion's all the entry fees go into the pot to be won by the players. In some cases the entry fee is $10,000. Binion's is profiting only from the publicity it will receive by sponsoring the tournament and providing the arena for this impressive contest.

The other well-known tournament, the Amarillo Slim Super Bowl of Poker conducted at the Sahara Tahoe casino-resort, is much like Binion's. There are many other smaller poker tournaments going on throughout the year, attracting the most skillful players from every state and even from other countries such as England, Ireland, and France.

For the astute player, or for the player who feels he is a bit beyond average (the best, perhaps, in his own group at home), these tournaments are a real boon. In such tournaments sometimes even amateur players can walk away with a lot of money.

Blackjack Tournaments

In the past five years, one casino game that has become a very popular tournament game is blackjack, or "21." This game is particularly big with younger gamblers, people in their twenties and thirties, who've learned that there is a way of playing blackjack, a certain strategy involved, which makes it somewhat a game of skill. In tournaments the players compete with one another, as well as with the house (as in roulette, craps, etc.). Here's how it works.

First of all, there are time limits on the tournaments (or a fixed number of hands to be played: one hundred) as well as restrictions on how much money is used. You will be eliminated from the competition or the round if and when you lose the original amount, which you have bought in for. You cannot replenish losses with fresh money; once the initial amount is lost—whether it be $500, $700, or whatever—the player is out.

The time limit is usually two hours to a playing session in a blackjack tournament. In two hours you can't really put together any great playing technique, especially when you're playing against the house and your fellow contestants at the table. So, luck and timing prevail in these tournaments.

Let's say there is a $35,000 blackjack tournament, with a registration fee and buy-in of $600. The players, seated together at random, are required to bet each hand with a minimum bet of $5 and a maximum bet of $500. Even if someone has amassed chips totaling $2,000/$3,000, the limit that person could bet would still be $500.

* * *

The object is to beat the dealer *and* the other players seated around the table. There is one winner per table; the player who wins Round 1 at the table advances to Round 2. The players who lose Round 1 are out of the game, unless—and this is a recent amendment—they wish to pay another registration fee and begin again. The winner is not required to pay any additional fee. Prizes are sometimes awarded to the winners of the round.

Round 2 continues much as Round 1, with the same betting

limits and rules. Players must keep their chips visible to the other players. At the end of the two-hour play, the person with the most chips is declared the winner.

At the end of a round, each player gets to keep the chips in front of him or her. So even if the other five players at the table are deemed losers of the round, they may still be ahead if they each finish with more than $600, which was the entry fee. At the end of the round, the chips are cashed in, because they are not good for any other game in the casino.

At the end of Round 3, the winners are in what is called the Championship Playoff, and eligible to win as much as $75,000 in cash. That winner will be awarded a champion title, and likely a beautiful trophy, as well as a considerable amount of prestige.

The winners of Rounds 1, 2, and 3 receive bonus prizes of $25,000, $40,000, and $60,000 respectively, and nine runner-up prizes are awarded. These may include complimentary accommodations in the casino's other hotels. Also, the player who accumulates the highest number of total winnings in all three rounds is awarded the title of Cumulative Winner and automatically advances to the Championship Playoff. Even if this player did not win any preliminary round, if his *total* winnings in all three rounds are higher than anybody else's, he wins the privilege of playing in the championship round.

* * *

Anyone with an eye to the big jackpot of a tournament should send away to the appropriate hotel or sponsoring casino for a rules brochure and read it over carefully. The rules are fairly easy to understand and therefore these tournaments attract a wide variety of people from all over; they provide an excellent opportunity to meet people in an exciting, high-rolling atmosphere.

These tournaments provide a great deal of fun and excitement for the few days of their duration, and they provide a lot of opportunities for players to win money and prizes. Reading gambling-related publications allows you to keep abreast of the various tournaments, rules, and dates.

Craps Tournaments

Craps tournaments are also very popular these days. The entrants are required to post a $250 entry fee, some of which is funneled into the prize pots.

Again, the table assignments for each player are randomly selected, with each player given an arbitrary number. The craps game is played the conventional way (see Chapter 1), with twelve to fourteen players assigned to each table. There is one round per hour. When the hour is up, whoever has the dice—the shooter—may finish his roll. The round does not end until that particular shoot is through.

Players must keep their chips in front of them, by denomination, in their racks. As in the blackjack tournaments, the minimum bet on a roll is $5, and the maximum is $500. On the proposition bets (like hard way 4, hard way 6, hard way 8, and hard way 10), 7, ace, ace-deuce, and 11, there is a $25 limit. On all other bets the limit is $500.

As in the blackjack tourneys, whoever wins Round 1 advances to Round 2. In some places, both the winner and the runner-up at each table may advance to the second round. Each player is given a receipt for his chips, which is cashed in at the end of the round. There are cash prizes awarded along the way to the winners of each round, as in the card tournaments.

Simple rules apply to the players: Keep your chips in view, hands off the table, etc. Courtesy and fair play are the name of the game.

* * *

The gaming tournaments, aside from providing fun and excitement for the players, also serve to promote the hotels and casinos that host them. They help to bring new faces to the scene, people who will return at a later date for another vacation.

Wherever you decide to play, remember to obtain the schedule and rules well in advance, enter as early as possible, have fun, and, hopefully, good luck!

10

OTHER GAMES

This concluding chapter illustrates and explains the basics of two games not covered in this book in greater detail: baccarat and the Wheel of Fortune.

When found in casinos, these games are usually few in number and receive the least amount of player participation, although baccarat is played for high stakes and usually represents significant swings in overall casino wins and losses.

The Basics of Baccarat: Simple and Elegant

The word *baccarat* is derived from the Italian *baccara*, which means "zero." The term refers to the face cards and the ten, all of which have zero value in the game of baccarat. In Europe, baccarat and a similar version called *chemin de fer* are among the most popular casino games.

Since baccarat's inception in Nevada, the game has assumed a glamour look. In most casinos, baccarat is played in a separate, roped-off area. The intention was to attract the high roller, or the more sophisticated, moneyed player. With the tuxedo-clad dealers, there is an elegance and aloofness to the game.

However, for all its enchantment, baccarat is primarily a simplistic game. There are no decisions or options: No degree of skill is required for either player or dealer. Players may sit in any open seat at the table; seating position does not affect the play in any manner. Each seat corresponds to a number on the layout, 1 through 15. Three dealers service the table. The dealer standing between positions 1 and 15 is known as the *caller*. He runs the game as cards are dealt from the shoe.

Each player gets a turn to handle the shoe. The player must bet the bank when he has the shoe, but any player may decline the shoe and it passes right along from player to player. Again, there is no advantage or disadvantage in dealing the cards; it's merely a formality and part of the ambience that players enjoy.

The caller receives the cards from the player with the shoe, places them in the appropriate boxes, and then calls for another card, or declares the winner, according to the rigid rules of the game.

Betting

Players bet by placing their chips in the numbered box opposite their seat. Bets may be made on the player or bank, and both are paid off at even money. In most games, bets range from a $20 minimum to a $2,000 maximum.

After the winner is announced, the two other dealers at the table pay off the winning bets and collect from the losers. If the *bank* was the winner, players who won must pay a 5 percent commission on their winnings. Thus, if a player had a $100 bet on the bank and it won, $5 would be owed to the house.

Rather than collect this *vigorish* after each game, a record of what is owed by each player is kept in a numbered box just opposite where the two payoff dealers sit. Players pay this accumulated amount after the finish of a shoe. Each time the shoe is depleted of cards, all eight decks are thoroughly shuffled and replaced in the shoe.

Determining the Value of the Hands

All cards, ace through 9, are valued according to their count. Tens and face cards count as zero. Thus, if the first two cards dealt are a king and a 4, the count is 4. An 8 and 6, although totaling 14, would come to 4 after subtracting 10. Here is a list of two-card and three-card totals to further illustrate the method of counting cards:

Cards	Hand Total
6, 5	1
4, 10	4
3, queen	3
8, 2	0
10, jack	0
9, king	9
8, 8	6
6, 4, 8	8
10, 4, 3	7
5, 2	7

When any two cards total over a 10-count, 10 must be subtracted. The remaining total is the card count.

Rules of Play

These rules apply in all American casinos; printed copies are available wherever baccarat is played. Dealers act according to these rules without consulting players at the table. The rules are automatic.

The highest total any baccarat hand can have is 9. A two-card total of 9 is called a *natural* and cannot lose. An 8 is the second-best hand and is also called a natural. If both player and bank are dealt identical hands, it's a *standoff* (a tie) and neither bank nor player wins.

No further cards can be drawn to a two-card draw of 6 or 7.

When holding other two-card totals, player and bank draw another card at the direction of the dealer, who does the calling. In studying the printed chart, one can easily determine the rules of the game.

It's a matter of letting the dealer do the calling, and declaring the outcome. Players are concerned only with how much they wager on each hand, and whether they bet on the player's side or the banker's. The house edge in baccarat is the lowest of any casino game. With only a 5 percent commission on winning bank bets, and nothing taken from winning player bets, the player's disadvantage is only 1.37 percent. In some casinos, players are permitted to bet on ties. The payoff is 8:1. It's a bad bet for the player, though, as the house edge is 14.1 percent.

Mini-Baccarat

A number of casinos have installed smaller baccarat tables, usually among the blackjack tables. It's the same game, but the rituals of passing the shoe, etc., are missing, and the game is staffed by one dealer. The layout, however, conforms to the regular baccarat table, and each seat position (1 through 6) corresponds to a numbered betting box (see diagram 10-1). Limits are usually from a $2 to $5 minimum up to a $500 maximum. Mini-baccarat is played fast, but the exact same rules apply as in the larger game.

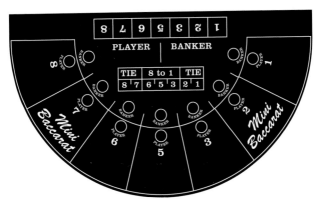

DIAGRAM 10-1

RULES:

Player	When first two cards total:
1–2–3–4–5–10	Draws a card
6–7	Stands
8–9	Natural–Stands

Banker	When first two cards total:	
Having	Draws when Player's third card is:	Does not draw when Player's third card is:
3	1–2–3–4–5–6–7–9–10	8
4	2–3–4–5–6–7	1–8–9–10
5	4–5–6–7	1–2–3–8–9–10
6	6–7	1–2–3–4–5–6–7–8–9–10
7	STANDS	
8-9	NATURAL—STANDS	

BACCARAT TERMINOLOGY

BANKER—The dealer hand in baccarat.

BANKER HAND—A bet that the hand called *banker* will come closer to 9 than the hand called *player*. Pays 11. A 5 percent fee is charged to all winning banker hands.

NATURAL—An 8 or 9 count in baccarat.

PLAYER—The player hand in baccarat.

PLAYER HAND—A bet that the hand called *player* will come closer to 9 than the hand called *banker*. Pays 1:1, with no commission charge.

PUSH—When hands tie in baccarat.

SKILL—A player employed by the casino who is usually at the baccarat table to help create the illusion of activity at an otherwise quiet table.

TALLY SHEETS—Slips of lined paper that enable players to keep a record of how hands are falling, and determine whether they are winning or losing.

TIE—A bet that both the banker and the player hands will tie. Pays 8:1. All bets on banker or player are considered a push in the event of a tie.

The Basics of the Wheel of Fortune
The Wheel

The game is known as the Big Six, or the Wheel of Fortune. It's another easy-to-play casino attraction, reminiscent of the old carnival wheels.

The wheel itself is made of wood in an elaborate and colorful design. Approximately six feet in diameter, the wheel is divided into nine parts, each part consisting of six identically spaced slots. There are exactly fifty-four of these slots separated by metal studs.

Positioned at the top of the wheel is a leather flap, and when the wheel is turning, a tick, tick, tick sound is heard as the strap hits against the nail-like metal studs.

Finally, as the wheel slows down, the strap will settle in one slot, and that particular one out of fifty-four slots will be declared the winner.

Betting

The slots are divided as follows: twenty-three $1 slots, fifteen $2 slots, eight $5 slots, four $10 slots, two $20 slots, and two slots that are joker or casino design slots.

Each of the slots carries the design of American currency, a $1 bill, for example, in each of the twenty-three $1 slots spread around the wheel.

A glass-covered table set in front of the wheel is where

players place their bets. Pieces of currency, one to match each of the denominations around the wheel, are represented on this betting table layout. Players place their bets on top of their selection. A bet on the $1 bill will pay $1 for an even-money return if the spin of the wheel results in the leather strap stopping in the $1-bill slot.

A bet on the $2 bill pays off at 2:1. The $5 winner gets 5:1, the $10 winner receives odds of 10 to 1, and 20 to 1 odds go to the lucky player who selected the $20 denomination (if the wheel should stop in either of the two slots marked with a $20 bill).

If the player selects one of the special designs or joker designate, the payoff is 40:1. Each of these 40:1 selections is an individual bet. In all, there are seven choices for making a bet.

Figuring the Odds

To calculate the percentage in favor of the casino, we multiply each payoff symbol by its dollar value, subtract that from the remaining total number of symbols, and divide by fifty-four. The $1 symbol gives us twenty-three chances of winning against thirty-one chances to lose. This leaves eight divided by fifty-four.

The casino edge is 14.8 percent. The fifteen $2 slots versus the thirty-nine other chances give the house an edge of 16.7 percent. The eight $5 symbols, paying 5 to 1 odds, give the house an edge of 11.1 percent.

The four $10 slots, paying off at 10:1, give the house an advantage of 18.5 percent. The two $20 slots, with odds of 20 to 1, still provide a built-in edge of 22.2 percent in favor of the casino. Either choice of a single bet on the joker or a special design slot works to a 24 percent house advantage.

Other combinations of denominations on the wheel will produce different house advantages . . . but now you know how to calculate the odds.

* * *

The attraction of the Wheel of Fortune is the aspect of fun and games. Patrons walking through the casino stop to watch the wheel as it spins and ticks, then stay to play a few dollars to see if their lucky guess produces a winner.

EPILOGUE: GAMBLING IS RECREATION

For 99 percent of us who visit a casino, racetrack, or card room, gambling is recreation. It is no different from attending a ballgame, a night at the opera, or a movie. It is to be enjoyed for a few hours, much like dinner at a favorite restaurant.

Unfortunately, there is always the temptation of too much of a good thing. Even though we are adults, some among us will take more than one helping of dessert; some will have to have "one more for the road, again." And, too, some will spend too much time and money gambling, taking a good thing too far.

If you (or people you know) have developed a compulsion to gamble—and it is affecting your life and the lives of those around you—there is help. And it is free.

The number to phone is 1-800-Gambler. Your identity and the content of your call will remain totally confidential.

* * *

Always remember, bet with your head, not over it.